THE BUSY PROFESSIONAL'S
GUIDE TO PASSIVE
REAL ESTATE
INVESTING

THE BUSY PROFESSIONAL'S GUIDE TO PASSIVE REAL ESTATE INVESTING

A PHYSICIAN'S PATH TO BUILDING WEALTH, CREATING FINANCIAL FREEDOM & LEAVING A LEGACY

VANESSA PETERS, MD

The publisher and the author do not make any guarantee or other promise as to any results that may be obtained from using the content of this book. Please note that much of this publication is based on personal experience and anecdotal evidence. You should never make any investment decision without first consulting with your own financial advisor and conducting your own research and due diligence. To the maximum extent permitted by law, the publisher and the author disclaim any and all liability in the event any information, commentary, analysis, opinions, advice and/or recommendations contained in this book prove to be inaccurate, incomplete or unreliable, or result in any investment or other losses. Nothing in this book is intended to replaced common sense or legal, accounting, or professional advice, and it is meant only to inform and educate.

For Griff and Mason—here's to our future adventures

Table of Contents

Introduction

A Tale of Two Doctors

Susan groans as the alarm chirps loudly, awakening her from a restless sleep. Morning already? She hasn't been sleeping well lately. She drags herself out of bed with a sense of foreboding, a generalized feeling of anxiety. She can't quite put her finger on what is bothering her.

As she drives to work in her late-model Mercedes, Susan finds herself dreading the day ahead. She's a busy family doctor; there are mountains of paperwork awaiting her attention. The extensive documentation in the electronic health record often takes longer than the patient encounter. Fighting with the insurance companies to provide appropriate care is another responsibility of the job. While she loves her patients, Susan often feels rushed and running behind, and this gets in the way of forming the meaningful connections that drew her to Family Medicine in the first place. She feels like she is not making the difference she hoped. Just another cog in the wheel of a big machine.

But I have a great life, she reminds herself. *I have a wonderful husband, two beautiful children, a lovely spacious luxury home in a gated community. The children attend a prestigious private school and we enjoy resort-style vacation several times a year.* This is the life she envisioned for herself. However, when she takes her family on vacation, she worries. While they deserve a nice trip, not only is it costly, but she doesn't have any income when she is not in the office seeing patients.

What is bothering her, she realizes during her thirty-minute commute, is that she feels trapped by the perfect life she has created. She makes a healthy six-figure income, but their bloated expenses and taxes leave a surprisingly small surplus, if any, at the end of the month. She contributes to her 401(k) plan, health savings account, and profit-sharing plan. Now in her forties with her retirement accounts only approaching the mid six-figures, she is starting to feel uneasy about her potential to save for a comfortable retirement. She is concerned about the lack of control she has over her nest egg, which is primarily in mutual funds. She knows she should be more involved, but honestly, she tries not to check the balance too often. The wild fluctuations in the stock market make her nervous. She knows that she needs at least four million dollars to retire with her current lifestyle. This would require her to work well into her late sixties. However, unlike so many of her physician mentors, she is not interested in working until she can no longer work.

She is a hamster on a wheel, running as fast as she can, but the destination never gets any closer.

Susan sighs, takes a deep breath and knocks on the exam room door to see her first patient this morning. This starts what is sure to be a jam-packed ten-hour day. She hopes that she can keep-on track. She has plans to go out this evening with her husband and does not want to work late at night, as she does most nights.

She pushes her anxiety and feelings of being overwhelmed deep down and puts on a bright smile to greet Mrs. Delaney. *Later,* she thinks. *I'll worry about my future later.*

Denise wakes up as the sun peeks over the horizon, excited and energized for another day. She meditates and does some gentle yoga before her family awakens. She relaxes with her coffee and enjoys time with her children before walking them to school, just a few blocks from their modest home.

Today she drives to her Family Medicine clinic, where she practices three days each week. Denise realized early in her career that living below her means would provide her with the freedom to tailor her work life to her needs. While no slouch, she understands that her older colleagues identified so strongly as "doctor" that it left little time for anything else except working sixty-hour weeks. Spending time with family, meaningful interests, hobbies, or travel all took a backseat.

Instead, Denise has thoughtfully and carefully plotted her path. While spending less than she made, she paid off her high-interest student loan debt first, kept expenses low, and started investing in real estate. While she contributes to a 401(k) for the company match, any additional money is funneled into creating passive income.

Rather than invest in active forms of real estates like flips, buy-and-hold single-family, or small multi-family homes, Denise skipped straight to investing passively in syndication real estate. While she loves real estate, she is smart enough to know that if she gets involved in finding, vetting and underwriting deals, overseeing construction, and being responsible for a home across the country, these tasks would take away from her precious limited time. The best use of her time is being a doctor, spending time with her family, and on activities that renew and invigorate her.

Denise is able to save $100,000 of her income annually for investing, despite not making as much money as her specialist colleagues, through her methodical planning. She invests this amount yearly and now after eight years is financially free.

This means she has choices. She has taken her hard-earned money and put it to work for her. Denise generates passive wealth twenty-four seven while she is sleeping, seeing patients, or on vacation.

She has built up her passive income such that it covers all of her basic expenses, allowing her to create a life that nourishes every part of her. Working part-time at the clinic, she is able to attend the last-minute events at her children's school and also volunteer in the classroom. She also spends time outdoors every day, a luxury she could not afford when working full-time. By creating the life she wants, the pace of her life is much more relaxed. Time seems to expand, instead of being a constantly panicked rush.

Denise loves travelling and plans several far-flung trips each year. She is excited to take a six-week sabbatical next year and explore Europe with her family. Even more than these experiences, being more available to her spouse and children has improved their relationships. They can sense her contentment and—as they say—happy wife, happy life!

She never thought that she would be so excited by life in her forties. Her life will just keep getting better and she's genuinely content and happy.

Chapter One

What Is NOT Passive Real Estate Investing?

L et's start with what passive real estate investing is *not*.

Many people are interested in real estate. They realize that investing in property can provide a path to wealth based on a physical asset. As the old adage goes, "Land, they're not making any more of it." However, as investing in real estate has become more popular, so have the courses, conferences, and TV shows that expound on all of the ways to get rich in real estate. You can go to a weekend conference to learn how to fix and flip homes. The Home and Garden Network shows you how easy it is to transform a house from drab to fabulous in a few weeks. Purchasing single-family homes to rent out is a very common way people enter the market. If your own area is too expensive, like where I live in San Diego, the next common step is to check out homes in other states—out-of-state investing.

Out-of-state investing is often done through a company that provides "turnkey" homes: houses that are renovated and ready to rent out. Sometimes it may even include the property management.

In my search for a way into the real estate market, I attended some local Meetups in San Diego. I encountered a lot of folks that were investing out of state. Some were buying in North Carolina, others in Ohio, Arizona, Florida or Texas. Anywhere but California (and New York). I could see the trajectory that they were taking. It was all about scaling your number of units. Getting more "doors."

I'll walk you through a typical scenario of a new real estate investor. The goal for many new investors is to use as little cash as possible, because they don't usually have much to start.

Purchase a single-family home or a small multiplex, like a duplex. Rehab it if needed to increase the value, rent it out and pocket the profits. If you can afford to purchase another one, great. Otherwise wait two to five years, then sell it and invest those proceeds into another, larger property, or do a 1031 Exchange.

A 1031 Exchange, or "like-kind exchange," is a way to take the equity from a real estate transaction and place it into another property in a defined period of time to avoid paying taxes on the profit. If you are able to exchange up to a four-plex then you have a more valuable property and more rental income. You've increased your door count. Again, in a few years, you can 1031 into another property, this time maybe a ten-to-fifteen-unit apartment building.

Other people will stick to the SFH (single-family homes) or small duplexes and purchase as many as they can. This can be up to ten, as the banks typically limit the number of mortgages an individual will qualify for.

Taking this path, which was what everyone I talked to was doing, didn't feel right to me. Investing in a property that was a plane ride away in an area I didn't personally know, with tenants that I wasn't picking, made me very nervous. Doing rehab on a property from afar scared the bejesus out of me too. Using one of the turnkey companies was an option to avoid the construction headaches, but the fact remained that I would be trusting a company and property manager that may not be aligned with my interests.

I'm very conservative with my investments. I work damn hard for my money and want to keep it safe. Personally, the risks of investing in a single property out of state were too much for me.

Another downside with any single family or small multifamily property is that a short vacancy can kill your profits for a year. You could find yourself paying mortgage, taxes and insurance on a place that is empty.

Speed Bumps on the Fast Track to Building Your Real Estate Empire

You'll likely encounter speed bumps—i.e., problems—if you build your portfolio the non-passive way. The first problem is finding the deal. If you want to find a home worth buying, you will spend a significant amount of time and energy scouring the resources available to you. I can attest to this. When I caught the real estate investment bug, I was determined to buy something—anything! I had a realtor friend start sending me homes for sale. I was getting an email from his MLS listing criteria about every five minutes. I was eager to check them all out; I was constantly distracted. Each time I got a new property email, I ran the investment numbers with an online calculator tool. The quick math people typically use to determine rental property cash flow is woefully inadequate. You need to add in property taxes, insurance, mortgage, utilities, capital expenses, vacancy rate, HOA or condo fees, and any miscellaneous expenses, not just the sale price. I was continually surprised at how little, or even negative, cash flow I would be getting from the properties that had initially looked promising.

Not only that, but I was not getting my *real* work done! It took about a week for me to realize that not only were there no deals in San Diego County. I was not able to find any deals, no matter where they were, maintain my sanity, and stay employed.

The second obstacle in growing your real estate empire is the amount of responsibility and work involved with directly owning a home/small multifamily. Flipping a home is a tremendous amount of work. If you're working full-time, all this responsibility needs to be outsourced. Otherwise you'll never complete the work in a timely fashion. Owning a rental property requires maintenance and upkeep, just like your primary residence. If the water heater or HVAC goes out, you need to replace it. If the roof needs replacing, there goes almost two years of profit.

The third obstacle is the vacancy rate. When you own a single-family home (SFH) you are either at 100% or 0% vacancy. If your place is empty, you are responsible for the mortgage until you get a tenant. This could potentially take away months of positive cash flow. And while "passive loss" sounds like it might be a good thing, think again. If you are a high-earning professional, you typically cannot deduct all of the losses because your income would be too high.

Oh wait, there is a fourth problem: property management. If you have, or are trying to have, a life and if your property is more than an hour away from where you live, you need to outsource your property management. Not only is this expensive (often 10% for SFH), but many of the property managers out there are not very good. Often their bread is buttered by having tenant turnover. They don't have any real incentive to keep your place occupied. They're not paying the mortgage. Topping it off, if they're out of state, you are really at their mercy.

And there is a fifth problem (I was way off on the number of problems): truly bad tenants. I'm talking about the ones that need to be evicted. The cost of evicting a tenant is going to squash your cash flow big time. Depending on the state, you will probably lose at least a few months' rent. But the place isn't just empty, collecting cobwebs. In this case, there is an unhappy tenant living there who is likely treating your beloved rental like crap. When they finally leave, you may be left with a mess to clean up that can top thousands of dollars.

Here's a true story that illustrates some of these speed bumps:

A couple of years ago I was determined to buy a property in my area. I found a small multifamily property with four units in my town. It was close to my work, it was affordable, and the rental calculator showed that it would bring in $1,063 per month. I felt that this property was going to start my real estate empire. I excitedly told my husband about it and showed him my glossy PDF document with pictures and projections.

I couldn't quite read him while I was explaining why this investment was such a good idea, but I got the distinct feeling he wasn't as excited as I was. He explained that there was absolutely no way we were going to purchase a run-down multiplex in "the ghetto" for him to take care of while I was busy working. I tried to explain that we could get property managers, but he countered with a story of when he was a kid cleaning up after tenants in that very area of town. His father had been a landlord and owned several working-class homes. My husband and his brother were responsible for cleaning up after tenants left. He recalled a time when tenants were evicted and there was crushed up macaroni ground into the carpet and the toilet was a hazardous waste area.

I will admit that I was pretty disappointed in his reaction. However, I knew that we needed to be on the same page. He was right, I would be putting a lot of responsibility on him. So, like water always finds a path, I started searching for another way to invest in real estate.

Chapter Two

What Is TRULY Passive Real Estate Investing?

A s I continued searching for ways to invest, I scoured Bigger Pockets, a real estate forum (www.biggerpockets.com). That site had several posts on *syndication*. What the heck was that? As it turns out, it is not related to *Seinfeld* reruns.

Syndication, in a Very Small Nutshell

Syndication is the pooling of resources to purchase a large asset, such as an apartment building. The investors are passive, limited partners (LP). The other partner is the General Partner (GP), also called a sponsor, operator or syndicator. The General Partner is the active partner that finds and analyzes the deal and creates the business plan.

Syndications are private placement investments. These types of investments are regulated by the Securities and Exchange Commission (SEC) under Regulation D, Rules (a), (b), and (c). Most of these investments require the investor to be accredited.

To be an accredited investor, a person must have an annual income exceeding $200,000, or $300,000 for joint income, for the previous two years with the expectation of earning the same or higher income in the current year. A person is also considered an accredited investor if he has a net worth exceeding one million, either individually or jointly with his spouse, excluding their primary residence.

You may be wondering, "How have I not heard about these types of investments?" The laws associated with the most commonly structured deals state that the offering must not be generally solicited or advertised. On top of this, the issuer, investment advisor or the broker-dealer, must have a *pre-existing substantive relationship* with any accredited investors. Therefore, you really have to know someone who is knowledgeable about syndications or stumble on them through your own research.

Dr. V's Step-by-Step Guide to Passive Real Estate Investing

Step One: Review. Once I become aware of a potential deal, typically in the commercial niches of multifamily (apartments), self-storage, or mobile home parks, I receive the Investment Summary, also known as a "deck," for review. The investment summary is 20–30 pages long and contains information about the deal. This is created by the General Partners. The deck is a colorful document with photographs and graphics to explain the deal, the market, financial projections and debt financing, the business plan, and to introduce the GPs and previous projects.

Step Two: Due Diligence. The next step is to perform due diligence on the details outlined in the deck. Research the operators, market, the building, and review the financial projections and assumptions. I usually make a few calls to people I may know in that market and speak to the operators. A recorded webinar done by the operator/general partner is always helpful to answer most of my questions. Sometimes I will fly out to view the asset myself.

Step Three: Invest. Once I have decided that this property is a good fit for my portfolio, I contact the investor liaison and advise them how much I would like to invest. This is also called "placing a soft hold," which is basically reserving your place in the deal while you continue to do your research and review the Private Placement Memorandum (PPM).

The PPM is a legal document required by the SEC. It tends to be 100 to 150 pages long. It contains a description of the offering, the risks and includes the partnership agreement, investment summary and subscription agreement. The entire PPM can be daunting and the risk section can be alarming, similar to a Surgeon General's warning or your latest prescription refill. It highlights every possible risk that could happen.

Much of the wording in the PPM is similar for any private placement and is mandated by the SEC, even down to the font size and bolding. The government wants to be sure that you are aware of all the facts, that this is not an insured investment and is not backed by any government agency. They are looking to protect us, the investors.

While it is true that there is risk with every investment, it's important to look at the track record of your sponsor and the history of these commercial investments in a severe downturn. The banks will not lend millions of dollars to a sponsor unless they have previous experience and have a solid business plan. The banks look for conservative underwriting, adequate insurance coverage, and a property condition report completed by outside experts.

After I have reviewed the PPM and completed my due diligence, I sign the PPM. This is almost always done electronically. Once signed, I can wire my funds to the operator. The wiring instructions are provided in the PPM. They are never provided by email for security purposes. It is safest and most expedient to wire funds instead of sending a personal or cashier's check.

Step Four: Relax! That's it for active participation on my part. Literally. Once I have wired the funds, I wait for a notification that the property has closed. Then I just sit back, relax, and smile as I get a direct deposit either monthly or quarterly directly into my account. The first check will usually be deposited sixty to ninety days after closing. I will get monthly updates advising me of the progress with the building and the operator will send quarterly reports with financials for my review.

Chapter Three

Time—Not Money—Is What You're After

O ur most precious resource is time. Time is the non-renewable resource that, once past, is gone forever. Many busy professionals provide a service for money. *TIME=MONEY*. When not working, professionals are not paid, whether they are taking a vacation, have an illness, or are going to their children's school assembly.

The biggest lesson I have learned is that time is a factor of whatever I do. Will this activity take up my precious time or will it help me create more time? Since we can't actually manufacture time, the next best thing is maximize our time. We all have the same twenty-four hours in a day, 168 hours in a week.

But time can do funny things. Do you remember as a child, waiting for Christmas or your birthday? Days seemed like weeks and hours seemed like days. Young people yearn for time to pass quickly so that they can reach milestones like the next grade or their sixteenth birthday. However, as we get older and busier, time seems to fly by at an alarming rate. Sometimes I feel like the time is speeding up as the weeks pass—another Monday already? How can it already be July?

The most common answer to the question "How are you?" is "Fine." But the next answer—sometimes even tacked onto "fine"—is "busy."

"Oh, thanks for asking. I'm fine, but busy." It's almost expected, really. Like it's a badge of honor to be too busy to enjoy your life. As if being busy is what is expected, a status symbol. But imagine instead this exchange:

"How are you?"

"Oh, thanks for asking! I am fantastic! I just had a leisurely breakfast, went for a hike and had lunch with a good friend. This afternoon I am going to relax, and maybe read a book or take a nap."

You would assume that the person responding to that question was retired, unemployed, or independently wealthy. This is because we expect any self-respecting person to be busy. They are busy to the point of fatigue, stress, anxiety, and lack of self-care. Busy people don't have time to exercise, eat well, get enough sleep, or relax with their friends and family.

Why are we so busy? There are multitudes of reasons we can't get into here, but a big one is *money*. We work very hard in our society, the United States in particular. We work for money to supply us with the essentials for life.

I went on a trip to Italy with my family recently. Several things struck me while we were there. One was that the Italians enjoy a distinctly different pace of life. Things moved much slower there. Eating was a several hour event, cappuccinos were sipped instead of gulped, and people moved at a leisurely pace. Even the airlines were slower; we quickly learned that the departure times were more like suggestions. Most planes departed about an hour or more after the expected time. The afternoons were a long siesta time for relaxing and resting. Our tummies on US time took a few days to accommodate to eating dinner at 9:00 p.m., at the earliest. Once we embraced it, the slower pace was calming. Your parasympathetic nervous system was activated, and, lo and behold, time seemed to slow down. When your sympathetic nervous system, your "fight-or-flight" response, is always on alert you feel rushed and on guard. Time will seem to slip away from you.

Physicians work hard for our money. There is no doubt about that. We worked hard to achieve our goals of becoming doctors with grueling training in medical school, residency, and fellowship. We lived lives of scarcity while in training, many of us racking up large student loans and debt. Due to long years of training we enter the workforce later than our peers. If you pursue a fellowship subspecialty, it is common to be in your mid to late thirties when you finish.

To make more money, you need to work longer or work harder. See more clients, patients, or complete more projects, all of which require your effort. To maximize your earning potential, you need to focus on activities that are the *highest and best use of your time*. However, even when you have optimized your time, there is still only one of you, and only twenty-four hours in a day. If you only focus on increasing your income by working more, other areas of your life will inevitably suffer—your health, your family and your sanity. All of this sacrifice will eventually making you wonder if you've chosen the right path.

How can you take your high earnings and leverage them to create financial freedom?

To me, financial freedom means that your basic expenses are covered if you cannot or choose not to work. To get there, you don't need to work harder, you need to work smarter by making your money work for you. So that when you are taking time away from your job (sleeping, traveling, relaxing) your money continues to generate income.

Chapter Four

Why Does Dr. V Invest Passively in Real Estate?

I was in practice for five years when I decided to divorce my husband in 2007, after nine and a half years of marriage.

The divorce process was slow. You must wait six months before any divorce is final in California. My lawyer and his lawyer exchanged letters until we finally decided on what seemed like a fair settlement.

Since California is a "no fault" state, and I wasn't willing to drag this out in court, we essentially split things 50/50. I agreed to pay him spousal support (alimony) for half of our marriage, or five years. This was a bitter pill to swallow, and I came to realize that the medicine was even more bitter because of how long I delayed taking it. In the spirit of getting through this, I agreed to give him my 401(k) in exchange for our home, which held some equity.

As the final divorce date approached, aligning with my thirty-second birthday, I saw a light at the end of the tunnel. I would not be deterred, even though my home value had gone down. I wasn't prepared for the bottom to fall out of the real estate market over the next six months. All across the country we watched our home values drop and soon I was deep underwater on my home that had lost half of its value.

Starting Over

I was overleveraged. As house prices soared it seemed like they would never stop going up. I treated my home like an ATM. I refinanced our home at 75% and when the friendly banker offered me a $200K home equity line of credit I was happy to accept. With the loan to value of my home at 84%, it turned quickly upside down. If I had planned on living there longer, I would have been able to weather the storm. Instead, I moved in with my boyfriend, and I became an accidental landlord. Fortunately, I lived nearby but I had a string of renters and frequent headaches. To top it off, the rent I received was short more than a thousand dollars of the expenses each month. Looking back, perhaps I should have sold via short sale right away, but I was hoping for a recovery. After five years of feeding the house and not seeing any way out, I did succumb to a short sale in 2012 with a mixed sense of relief and failure.

Fortunately, during this time, I took the advice of a realtor friend and purchased an investment property in Riverside County, thirty minutes north of my home. It was a short sale of a newish home and in great condition. I was initially excited but then a little disillusioned as prices continued to fall for another year or so. I was not educated enough about real estate to understand that this was the time to buy more properties, so I held on to the one. Once I had good renters, I "set it and forget it." It has been a cash-flowing, trouble-free property for over ten years. I just wish I had purchased ten of them.

Around this time, I also made one of the best investments ever—a good financial team. My team consists of experts to help me with my taxes, estate planning, accounting, and investing. They are a team of financial planners, a CPA, and a lawyer. As a professional with a relatively high income, it is imperative to get the advice of professionals who can help you maximize your income, reduce taxes, and provide shelters from taxes. Especially living in California!

I was in my early thirties when I started with this team. After I had been with them for several years, I was feeling pretty good about my savings rate and my increase in net worth. The stock market was on a bull run and things were looking good. I was qualified as an "accredited investor" and felt that I had done quite well considering starting over just a few years prior.

Living with my new fiancée, I wanted to enjoy as much of my new life as possible. I realized that I wasn't willing to work, with my nose to the grindstone, until I was retirement age. I wanted to travel, enjoy life, and spend time with loved ones! I had to make up for lost time.

As my team gathered for our annual tax planning session, I boldly stated, "I want to retire when I'm forty-five." Looking back, I can see they were suppressing a smile from the naïve thirty-five-year-old in front of them.

"Do you know how much you need to retire, taking into account inflation, and assuming a withdrawal rate of four percent?" my advisor asked gently.

"Well, no," I stammered.

"You will need about five million dollars to have an income of $120K per year in retirement."

My jaw dropped. At my current savings rate, forty percent of my income, I was on track to be working well into my sixties, a far cry from retiring at forty-five. Even if I stepped it up, saved more than half my paycheck, and lived frugally, it would only move the needle a little, by a few years.

Dejected, I gave up on the idea of retiring in ten years and went back to work. Over the next five years I saved diligently, worked hard, and followed instructions. While I was generally frugal, I had a baby boy in 2011 and a strange thing happened. On my maternity leave I learned the dark side of being a mom, for me anyway: the allure of Babies "R" Us, and Amazon. While I was no stranger to shopping, having a little bundle of joy to purchase for changed everything! Of course, he needs another little primary-colored toy that he can't even hold yet! Of course, he needs another pair of perfectly adorable booties that don't stay on. Of course, he needs the cutest little collared shirt that will be soiled with spit up in minutes. In my dazed, sleep-deprived state the baby marketers had me by the (bouncy) balls.

Fortunately, I was not destined to be a stay-at-home mom; it was not a good idea for me. I am much more disciplined and productive when I'm busy with work, not shopping for baby tchotchkes.

I have many interests, serial interests you could say. When I become interested in a topic, I delve deep, bordering on obsession, until I have learned all I can about it. Then, typically, I move onto another topic. I have done this with yoga, various food related topics, and homesteading: chickens, fermenting, gardening, and organizing (shout out to Marie Kondo).

Around my fortieth year, I became disillusioned with my financial situation. Since my chat about finances with my team five years earlier, I had been diligently saving, using all of the tax advantaged vehicles available to me and being generally frugal, except for the "baby year." I was concerned whenever I reviewed my net worth. While I was making progress, the upward trend was worryingly linear. I had heard so much about compound interest, but I didn't see it working for me in a meaningful way.

I was investing in stocks, mutual funds and bonds, as directed, and I had a few real estate investments. I decided to double down and work to save even *more* money.

This next bit is a cautionary tale.

As is typical for me, I delved deep into frugality over the following year. I took out scores of books from the library with titles like *Save and Grow Rich*, *Frugal Living*, and *How to Live on $100 per Month*. Just kidding on that last one, but you get the idea. This is a real book I studied: *America's Cheapest Family Gets You Right on the Money*. I learned about FIRE (Financial Independence Retire Early). I became convinced that if we would just stop spending money, and saving it instead, that was the path to financial freedom and security. Of course, since I have a family, this brand of extreme frugality was also imposed on them. This was met with some pushback. I found myself getting frustrated and disillusioned with the spending habits of my husband and would interrogate him on why he felt the need to purchase, well, anything.

I turned my obsession next to our energy costs. We had solar panels, but we were utilizing more electric than they produced and I wanted to know why. I am embarrassed to admit that I spent a week checking the energy utilization of all of our appliances, and anything that plugged in. I spent hours tracking our total usage in a spreadsheet. I thought I was doing this on the down low, but my husband got completely fed up with me and told me to get some help. That was a wake-up call. I was truly obsessed with what amounted to no more than fifty dollars each month of variance in our electric bill, spending countless hours analyzing and thinking about it. He was right, and I did get some help. With a wonderful therapist, I was able to let that go.

That was a much-needed wake-up call. Since then, a vacation in Minnesota a few summers ago changed my life trajectory.

It was a beautiful warm mid-July morning in Minnesota. I was taken by surprise with a feeling of complete and utter contentment. I was bicycling with my family around a lake on a smooth, groomed gravel path surrounded by trees and ferns, in so many shades of green my breath was taken away. The cool riparian air mixed with the warmth of the sun and the laughter of children up ahead floated toward me. The quiet crunching of tires on gravel was meditative. I had a sudden realization.

I need more of *this* in my life. I want to be with my family and my son while he is young. We only have 536 Saturdays before our children are eighteen, grown and out in the real world. That is not enough time! In our society, we spend our prime years, when we are healthy, full of energy, and at the top of our game, with our job. We want to contribute, have purpose, and do great things, but we also need to take time for ourselves, before it's too late.

The idea of waiting for retirement to really relax and enjoy ourselves, to take that time or that big vacation, is outdated. We need to take those adventures and experience them now, during our most valuable years. But, how? My dilemma, and that of many professionals, is that we exchange time for money. We provide a professional service and are compensated for this. However, many of us are not compensated unless we provide that service. If we don't see patients, clients, or work on that project, then we don't get paid.

If you take a trip to Machu Picchu and spend a month touring South America you'll have a wonderful time, amazing memories, and strong quad muscles. For the high-earning professional, when you return you will see a dip in your income that may affect you for months. This explains why many of us don't even take the offered time-off in our jobs. We can't afford to suffer the drop in our income.

Some of us may not have wanderlust, but just want more time away from the office. Working part-time is a pipe dream for many.

Getting Clear About What Money Means to You

What is this life really about? What do we really want? Is it money or is it what money can give us? What makes you happy and content? Discontent occurs when you have a sense of lack. Something is lacking in your life. When you are truly content, everything is okay, and your desires are satisfied. This is our true nature, our center. This doesn't mean that you can't still aspire to achievements, goals, and dreams. Those are what makes us human.

When it really comes down to it, I need to be careful about the pursuit of money for money's sake alone. What money affords me is the freedom to pursue activities, travel, and take time with friends and family. That is the *what* I need to pursue, the ability to purchase comforts that make my life better, give me mental space to create, and let me be content without worry.

What vehicle can provide the money that we seek as well as balance with the time spent? Short of starting a company that goes public making you a zillionaire, what can you do? I don't like to work in improbabilities. I don't have any special talents, or ideas for inventions, and I will never be a famous anything. Understanding that we need our money to make money for us so that our time is free is the Holy Grail.

My path to finding passive income with real estate reignited that day on the bike path in Minnesota. I marvel at how a single incident can take you in ways you never expected or could plan for.

After our trip, I wanted badly to recreate the experience of leisurely riding bikes around a lake. Where we live in Southern California, we have a shortage of lakes and nice flat bike paths. We've got the ocean, of course, but that isn't the same feeling of relaxation. I started thinking about getting a vacation home to Airbnb in Lake Tahoe. I've never been there but have heard great things. A new obsession was born. I started reading everything I could about real estate. I refreshed my memory with some *Rich Dad, Poor Dad* books. I had read those when I was fresh out of residency but wasn't in a headspace where I was going to give up my newly minted MD for a business/investor mindset. Plus, at the time I was heavily in debt and that all seemed impossible.

I went to Bigger Pockets, an online forum with tons of real estate resources and information. I took the limit of ten books out of the library. I lived and breathed real estate. My husband, noting the plethora of books around the home, concluded that I was onto a new idea that would burn out in a few months. He listened politely as I excitedly told him my findings.

I even found a turnkey Airbnb rental for sale in South Lake Tahoe. It was a stretch to buy it, but it was already successful, and I was seriously considering it when I hit a roadblock. The short-term rentals are limited in the town and the wait for a permit was expected to be two years. Okay, so that won't work. My original plan of riding a bike around a lake to recreate the experience was just a jumping-off point for a much bigger idea.

I began scouring the local market for a deal in San Diego and Riverside County. It didn't take me too long to figure out a couple of things. One, there are really no good cash flowing properties in the area. Two, I should not be hunting for deals.

So, I kept looking. Like water always finds a way, I had a feeling there was a way I could invest in real estate without spending too much time or taking big risks. The first time I read the word *syndication* on a real estate forum, I ignored it. That word had no context for me, except in relation to old reruns so I disregarded it. But I came across it again, and again.

Fine! I thought to myself. *What the hell is this? I better figure it out.* The concept of syndication seemed to be shrouded in mystery, and a quick web search left me befuddled. So, I reached out to a member of BP who was posting answers to questions about syndication, seemed fairly knowledgeable, and had a legit website. When I spoke with him on our introductory call, he explained the basic nuts and bolts of syndication.

Chapter Five

What is Syndication, Really?

S yndication, in its simplest form, is a group of investors coming together. Typically, the investment is led by a few General Partners, also known as sponsors or key principals. While real estate is not the only type of investment done with syndications, that is the focus of this book and we won't go into other types of investing here. But as an example, syndications can be done with businesses (restaurants) and livestock to name a few.

The Meat and Potatoes of Syndication

In real estate, the General Partner (GP) will find a property to purchase. This can be any type of real estate, from commercial retail, to bundles of single-family homes, to apartments, self-storage facilities and mobile home parks. We will be focusing on the last three types of real estate here. Once the property is under contract—their offer has been accepted—the GP will reach out to their investors, or Limited Partners (LP), to raise the capital needed to fund the deal. Since most syndications are large investments, from one to $60 million, the GP will get a mortgage for a portion of this, usually 60–75%. The remaining amount is the Capital Expenditures Budget (CapEx) and is needed for the down payment and the construction budget for improving the building.

The role of the Limited Partner is just that—limited. The General Partner is the active one. They find the deal, develop relationships with brokers, analyze many deals a week to see if they might be profitable, perform the underwriting and the due diligence, and create a business plan.

The Limited Partner does not have a say in how the business plan should be implemented, or even what it includes. The benefit of this is limited liability. You, as the LP, have no responsibility regarding the operations of the property, or if someone is injured on the property. Your risk is limited to the money you've invested. The beauty of this is that you receive income from real estate, without actually doing any work.

Adding Value: The Long Flip

The business plan of most of these opportunities is to add value. The goal of purchasing an asset such as an apartment building is to improve it over several years and sell it for a profit. It's easy to visualize this process as a long "flip." Most of us are familiar with the idea of flipping a home. As discussed earlier, this is a very active form of investing in real estate.

For a 250-unit apartment building, the principle is the same. Purchase a building that is in need of some improvements, ideally an asset from the 1980s that is structurally sound but needs to be updated. The areas that syndicators look at improving in apartment buildings, for example, include upgrading the kitchens to granite countertops, laminate flooring, new faucets, lighting and modern cabinets.

The color schemes of carpet, cabinets and wall paint are modernized. Sometimes keyless entry and Nest thermostats are installed. Amazon lockers may be placed in the clubhouse to enable residents to pick up their packages at their convenience, instead of being limited to when the office is open.

Covered parking is at a premium in the southern states, so this can be added. Adding a small fenced-in yard to the first-floor units is a big selling point for pet owners. Updating the clubhouse décor, renovating the on-site gym to have good airflow, the newest cardio machines and televisions, is another benefit to the residents. The playground and landscaping are improved, and the exterior may be painted. Many older apartment buildings have plenty of opportunity for improvement, and thus an opportunity to return your investment.

It is important that the improvements are things that will provide obvious value to the residents. For example, if the roof, plumbing, or electrical need work these expenditures will not increase rents. Residents expect these things to be working, at absolute minimum. That's why selection of a building that has good "bones" is so important, with only superficial improvements needed.

The syndicator looks out for properties that have "meat on the bone," meaning that there are significant improvements to be made that will increase the rents of the building. This is a win-win situation for the General Partners, the investors, and the tenants.

The GP are not going into a building and raising rents without providing value. The tenants are usually pleased that the new landlord wants to give them a nicer building to live in and will pay the increased rent. It is also important to be competitive with the other buildings nearby, ideally a little below the market rent. This provides security to the investors for several reasons.

One aspect of that security is keeping the building well occupied, a target of about 95%, and the other is to provide protection in a financial downturn. If you own the new development built in 2010, which though nice, is also quite expensive, what happens if the economy falters? Many residents will need to move out of their premium apartments and move into a less expensive place. They will be looking for the 1980s vintage building with updated amenities (our place).

In addition to adding value as described above, the GP will also work to decrease expenses and streamline processes. Typical expenses include the property manager salary, utilities, landscaping, and maintenance. Creating efficiencies can reduce overall expenses. When an operator has several buildings in the same area they can also use economies of scale.

Getting Good Grades

Both properties and locations are graded A/B/C/D. An A class property is a new development built in the last ten to fifteen years. B class properties were built in the last fifteen to thirty years. C class properties are older than thirty years (1980s or older, at the time of this writing) or run-down newer buildings. D class buildings are, basically, the ghetto.

The location mirrors this classification. A areas are places with good schools, parks, bike paths, new shopping centers with nice grocery stores and coffee shops. B areas are still nice but not as new. C areas are working-class neighborhoods with older amenities and less green space. A D class area is one that, if you drove through it, would make sure your doors are locked and not feel safe getting out. Crime and drug use are common in D class areas, and they are lacking in basic amenities like grocery stores.

Investing in a B or B- property in an A class area is ideal, with good potential for profit while being safe. Investing in a C class property may have more potential, but there is more risk. Investing in a C class area is risky. The rationale for investing here relies heavily on what the area might do. As C class areas gentrify, their values increase significantly, apart from the value-add propositions outlined above. However, predicting what areas are in the path of progress can be tricky. It may look like an area is going to explode with hipsters, Starbucks, and gastropubs only to have the path of progress take a right hand turn right before the property, leaving the investment in a precarious position.

Another important aspect is the market and submarket. The market is extremely important. We will get into more detail later regarding this but suffice it to say that you want to be in a market that is growing with both jobs and people. Primary markets are best; look for larger cities, compared to secondary or tertiary markets. There are lower prices in the other markets but it's more difficult to increase rents and keep occupancy up, which makes it riskier.

What's It Worth to Ya? A Primer on the Valuation of Commercial Properties

Let's talk about valuation—what a property is worth to you—or, more accurately, the bank. This is super important; the way that we have learned to value our personal properties is much, much different than commercial real estate. For a single-family home, up to four units or quad-plex, the valuation is based on comparable homes in the market, or "comps." As anyone knows who has purchased or sold a home, the value of your home is at the mercy of the market comps. I know it feels unfair to have your home appraised and valued compared to homes in the vicinity that have no more in common than approximate square footage and number of bed and baths. However, the fact is that the uniqueness of your place is largely irrelevant when it comes to valuation in the residential market.

My personal residence is a good example. It is an older home, built in the 1960s as a ranch style home in Southern California. My husband poured a year of his life into renovating this home. He took it down to the studs and rebuilding almost completely, including a beautiful addition, wide open rooms, and lovely mahogany and teak throughout. We also converted an old rat-infested standalone garage to a climate-controlled room and music studio. The half-acre property has been fully fenced with electric gates, and truckloads of massive boulders and native plants were imported. A koi pond provides relaxing white noise. In spite of all of this, at the end of the day, when we have our home appraised, it is actually worth less than our neighbors' property, who have done no upgrades. Doesn't seem fair, does it?

If you are thinking about doing a home improvement to increase the value of your home, beware. Most of the time the money spent on upgrading the kitchen or bathroom is not recouped when the home is sold. Most realtors recommend upgrading for yourself, not to make big bucks on the sale.

Here is the good news. For commercial real estate, five or more units, valuation is a totally different animal. Instead of passively waiting for the market to rise in value, in commercial buildings you can force appreciation.

This is an extremely important concept and is the reason that buying this kind of real estate is so profitable. Remember the single-family house flipper? They are also forcing appreciation by making huge improvements in a short time and selling before the market appreciates (except in very hot markets). But the secret weapon of commercial real estate is the way valuation is calculated. Instead of using comps, they use a calculation of Net Operating Income (NOI) divided by the Capitalization rate (cap rate).

The capitalization rate (cap rate) is simply what investors should expect to earn if they paid 100% cash for an asset. Example: if an apartment costs one million dollars and the cap rate is 6%, then the investor should expect to get 6% annually or a return of $60K, from the investment. The capitalization rate is determined by the market and is location specific. As a rule, the higher the cap rate, the lower the cost of the building, the easier it is to make a profit. The lower (or compressed) cap rates occur in very expensive cities like New York, Los Angeles and San Francisco. It is very difficult to find an investment that will make money in a low cap rate environment.

Some investors and syndicators have criteria for cap rates. For example, they won't invest in anything with a cap rate lower than 7%. But that may be too simplistic as there are many factors that make a deal worthwhile.

The Net Operating Income is the income that is brought into the property annually, through rents and ancillary services, minus the costs associated with running and renovating the property. The beauty of this, and the valuation calculation, is that you can:

Increase income through value-add strategies outlined above.

Decrease expenses by creating efficiencies.

Both of these increase your NOI, and just a small change in the NOI is expanded when you divide by the cap rate, expressed in percentage.

The Powerful Force of Forced Appreciation

Here's an example of how we can force appreciation. In a 300-unit apartment building acquired last year, we identified a desire for covered parking. About two-thirds of residents agreed to pay the modest $25 monthly fee for covered parking, bringing in approximately $5000 each month or $60K per year. The cost of building the covered parking was $90K. In about eighteen months we would break even.

But more importantly, the value of the apartment increased by one million dollars, effectively adding one million in equity. Increase of NOI $60K/6% cap rate (0.06) = $1,000,000. What seems like a very small increase in income—$25 per unit—translates to a very large amount of value.

If, for the same 300-unit apartment building, we were able to increase rents across the board by $100 per unit, a conservative amount, this would result in $100 x 285 (assuming 95% occupancy) or $28,500 per month. This adds up to $342,000 per year. Divide this sum by the cap rate of 6% and we have added $5.7 million in equity, of increased value.

	Covered Parking	Global rent increase
Increase per unit	$25	$100
Number of Units	200	285
Increase in income	200x $25 = $5000/month Or $60,000/year	285 x $100 = $28,500/month Or $342,000/year
Cap Rate	6%	6%
Annual Income/cap rate = increase in equity	60000/0.06 = $1,000,000	342000/0.06 = $5,700,000

When I first saw this, I thought it seemed like funny math, or something illegal. I can tell you now, this is completely legit. It is how commercial valuation is done all day, every day.

I have focused on apartments in this example for illustration purposes, but the same principles apply to self-storage and mobile home parks, which I will touch on later.

Show Me the Money: Dr. V Does the Math

So now that you know what a syndication apartment deal is, you may be wondering: what does it really mean to be a Limited Partner in a syndication deal? How do I get paid, and when?

This varies based on the deal, but there are several common structures, which we will outline here.

Limited Partners (LP) invest anywhere from $25,000 up to several million dollars but the most common investments amounts are $50–$150K.

The LP receive a preferred return which will be paid monthly or quarterly. This typically ranges from 6–8% but can be higher or lower. The preferred return is paid to the LP before the GP receives any income.

Sample $100,000 investment scenario:

- Assumptions
- 8% preferred return
- 20% cash-on-cash return including sale of property
- Five year hold period

Investor Returns Based on a $100,000 Investment						
	Investment	Year 1	Year 2	Year 3	Year 4	Year 5
Investor Annual Percent Returns		8%	8%	8%	8%	168%*
Investors Return on Investment	($100,000)	$ 8,000	$ 8,000	$ 8,000	$ 8,000	$ 168,000
Total Return over 5 years including return of initial investment						$ 200,000

*includes return of equity

Note that the preferred return is cumulative. This means that if the operator is not able to pay the preferred return one year, they add it to next year's returns. For example, it is possible that the LP has an 8% preferred return but the operator, due to construction costs and stabilizing the property in the first few years, is unable to pay the full 8% in years one and two. In this case, if they pay 4% during years one and two, they would owe 16% in year three. This is because in year one they were short 4%. This is then added to year two (8% + 4% = 12%). If they only pay 4% again in year two then they would then owe 16% by year three (8% + 4% + 4% = 16%). See the illustration, below.

Investor Returns Based on a $100,000 Investment						
	Investment	Year I	Year 2	Year 3	Year 4	Year 5
Investor Annual Percent Returns		8%	8%	8%	8%	168%*
Investor Actual Returns		4%	4%	16%	8%	
Return owed to investor (cumulative)		4%	12%	16%	8%	
Investors Return on Investment	($100,000)	$ 8,000	$ 8,000	$ 8,000	$ 8,000	$ 168,000
Total Return over 5 years including return of initial investment						$ 200,000
					*includes return of equity	

The preferred return continues to accumulate until it is caught up, either during the life of the project or on the sale. Frequently an operator will do a refinance or supplemental loan after the property is fully stabilized, with all value-add opportunities realized and occupancy at the target level. This often occurs in the third year of ownership.

The operator goes back to the bank, shows them the new NOI, resulting in a significant amount of equity which can be pulled out through refinance. This equity is returned to the limited partners and includes the catch-up of the preferred return. The tax benefits of this are important. The money returned to the investors is considered "return of capital" and is therefore not a taxable event. This is a great benefit to the passive investor, who will have access to a large portion of the principal invested in the deal. That capital can then be reinvested in another deal, or for whatever they wish. And the best part is that you continue in the original deal, receiving your preferred returns for the life of the investment.

How the General Partnership Is Paid

The General Partners work very hard to scour the market for deals, develop relationships with brokers and analyze projects daily to determine if they are worth purchasing. Countless hours are spent developing a business plan, underwriting, running the numbers and getting financing. The operators understand that without capital, there is no deal. So, they want the investment to be a win for both sides, the LP and the GP. In a good deal this is most definitely the case.

Fees. Acquisition Fee: this ranges from 1-3% of the purchase price of the asset

Asset management fee: this also ranges from 1–3% of the ongoing income, paid monthly.

The Split. Apart from the acquisition fee and asset management fee, the General Partners also share in the profits after a few hurdles are reached. This applies to all distributions and capital events. The Limited Partners receive all of the profits until their preferred return is reached. After that the profits are split, generally in favor of the LP. A very common split is 70/30, with 70% to the LP and 30% to the GP. Remember, this is after the preferred return is fully caught up and paid to the LP.

Some deals have a change in the split once a certain Internal Rate of Return (IRR) is reached. For example, the 70/30 split changes to 50/50 after an IRR of 13% is met. This is called a "waterfall."

In the next chapter we'll drill down into the most commonly asked questions about passive real estate investing through syndications.

Chapter Six

More Answers to Your Questions About Syndications

Definition of *syndication*

1**:** an act or instance of forming a <u>syndicate</u> or bringing something under the control of a <u>syndicate</u>

> //real estate syndication

2a: the act of selling something (such as a newspaper column or television series) for publication or broadcast to multiple newspapers, periodicals, websites, stations, etc.

> //the syndication of news articles and video footage

2b: the state of being syndicated to multiple newspapers, periodicals, websites, stations, etc.

> // a popular TV show that has made millions in syndication

From <https://www.merriam-webster.com/dictionary/syndication>

Here are some of the most common questions asked by passive investors learning about syndication. These questions are focused on value-add apartment syndication.

1. What is syndication?

    Syndication is the pooling of resources to purchase a large asset, such as an apartment building. The investors are passive, Limited Partners (LP), and the General Partner (GP), also called a sponsor or syndicator. The General Partner is the active partner that finds, analyzes and creates the business plan.

2. Who can invest in a syndication deal?

    These types of deals are marketed under SEC regulations 506(b). This means that the deals can be shared with accredited investors only with whom we have a prior relationship.

3. What is an accredited investor?

    To be an accredited investor, a person must have an annual income exceeding $200,000, or $300,000 for joint income, for the last two years with expectation of earning the same or higher income in the current year. An individual must have earned income above the thresholds either alone or with a spouse over the previous two years. The income test cannot be satisfied by showing one year of an individual's income and the next two years of joint income with a spouse. The exception to this rule is when a person is married within the period of conducting a test. A person is also considered an accredited investor if he has a net worth exceeding one million, either individually or jointly with his spouse, excluding his primary residence.

4. What is a Limited Partner (LP)?

    The limited partner is a passive investor in the deal. They have limited liability and their risk is limited to the amount that they have invested, no more. All other assets are protected. They cannot be sued, are not listed on the loan and, best of all, they are not responsible for any active management of the property.

5. What kind of returns can I expect from an apartment syndication?

   Typical returns are 8-10% annually with an internal rate of return (IRR) of 16-22%. The average rate of return is obtained by taking the total return over five years divided by five. This is typically higher because it does not take into account the time-value of money, as the IRR calculation does.

6. What is a preferred return?

   The "Pref" or preferred return is the percentage given to the limited partners first, before the general partners are paid. This is typically 8%. This means that the first 8% return on an investment will go entirely to the limited partner. After the LP are paid, then the General Partner will start to receive distributions as well. This helps align interests with the General Partners.

7. When will I get paid?

   After the property closes, distributions begin approximately two months later. The preferred return is paid either monthly or quarterly. These distributions can be directly deposited into your bank account.

8. What kinds of tax implications are there to this kind of investment?

   Fortunately investing in real estate is tax-advantaged, and syndication is no different. The sponsor will be deducting property taxes, loan interest and depreciation and you will benefit from this as well. The depreciation is accelerated since the asset is not held for more than five to seven years. You will receive a K-1 statement from the general partnership in March. It's not unusual for the K-1 to show a paper loss, despite a monthly or quarterly income, on average $8000 on a $100K investment. Even better, any supplemental loans or refinance events are reviewed as a "return of equity," so they are not taxable events.

   And lastly, at the time of sale of the property, there may be an opportunity to do a 1031 Exchange into another property that the sponsor purchases, thereby deferring your capital gains.

9. What is a supplemental loan?

   When the property is purchased, the GP will start to add value to the property as outlined in the business plan. This is done through renovations, improving operations, decreasing expenses, and increasing rents as improvements are completed. Since a commercial property is not valued on comparable properties, as in residential real estate, the value is calculated based on net operating income (NOI) divided by the local capitalization rate, or "cap rate." When the value of the property is increased, the GP can return to the bank with a higher value and either refinance the property or obtain a second loan on the property. This is called a supplemental loan. This allows you to pull out equity from the investment, which is returned to the investors. This typically occurs after the units have been renovated, which takes two to three years on average.

10. What is the timeline and process of a typical syndication deal?

    Once a property is under contract, due diligence takes about sixty days. The investment summary, or deck, is completed, and a conference call is recorded. The investors are notified of the deal and the operator raises the needed funds over approximately six weeks, spending time educating investors about the deal. Interested investors reserve a spot, review the offering (sign the subscription agreement in the PPM), and fund the investment. About two to four weeks later they close on the property. About 45 to 120 days later, the first investor distribution occurs.

Syndication Timeline (60-90 Day Closing Cycle)

Equity Raise
-Investment summary and PPM assembled
-Conference call scheduled

Investor Commitments
-Sponsor meet with investors to answer further questions
-Investors may reserve a spot

Property Close
-Deal funded
-Sponsor takes control of property

Investor Distributions and Updates
(60-90 days after close)

Property Under Contract

Due Diligence
-Property inspections
-Financial analysis
-Value-add strategy

Conference Call
-Investors can email questions to Sponsor
-Sponsor shares deal

Investor Action
-Investors sign PPM
-Funds wired

11. What is the typical holding period for this type of investment?

We target five years for most deals. At that time the original principal invested as well as any profits are distributed. Sometimes it makes sense to sell in year three, but if a downturn occurs the hold time can be increased to seven years. There is no rule that the property must be sold in five years, even if the market is down. This protects your investment.

12. What if there is a downturn in the economy?

As described above, we would not sell in a down market, but rather hold the property and continue to pay the preferred return to the Limited Partners. Fortunately, apartments are protected during a downturn for several reasons. Class B assets hold their value and occupancy rates because people moving out of homes or more expensive apartments need affordable housing. Our rents are targeted below the top of the market for this reason. In the downturn of 2008, the rental income from apartments only decreased 5% while the residential market values decreased 34%.

13. What are the risks of apartment syndication?

The risks are outlined in the Private Placement Memorandum (PPM). This document is 100 plus pages long and much of the wording is regulated strictly by the SEC, down to the placement of the text and the font. This is to educate the investor. This type of investment is not insured or protected by the government. However, the strength of the syndication team is of utmost importance. If your team has strong partners and a proven strategy to add value to apartments in good neighborhoods your risk is lessened. Even the money we place in mutual funds or the stock market is not insured or protected. We don't sign a PPM to place money in Wall Street, but maybe we should.

14. Does the syndicator or sponsor invest in their own deal?

To promote alignment of interests many sponsors will invest alongside the Limited Partners on the LP side of the deal.

15. What is the minimum investment?

Most deals have a $50K minimum investment and increments of $5K thereafter.

16. Can I get my money back before the property is sold?

This type of investment should be considered illiquid. Having said that, if you encountered a hardship, many operators would work with you if possible.

17. Is it possible to utilize a 1031 Exchange into a deal?

No, you cannot 1031 into the deal, but it may be possible to use the 1031 Exchange to move into another deal with the same operator.

18. Can I use a Self-Directed IRA or Solo 401(k) to fund this investment?

Absolutely! One of the best ways to build wealth is to maximize your tax-deferred vehicles to invest in real estate. This allows you to keep the proceeds from the investment tax-free as well until withdrawal (or forever, if you use a Roth). The SD-IRA has something called UBIT tax whereas the 401(k) does not.

19. How is the property renovated while people are living there?

When the property is taken over, there will be vacant units even if the occupancy rate is at 95%. For example, in a 400-unit building there would be twenty vacant units. The renovations are started on those empty units, rents are raised following the improvements. The following month, when leases are coming up, the newly renovated units will be offered to those residents who are renewing and start renovating their vacated unit along with any other units that are vacated. This is repeated until all of the units are renovated. Ideally, the improvements are so dramatic that retention and new lease signups will be high.

20. What is the timeline of purchasing an apartment building?

Once the property is under contract, the due diligence phase lasts about sixty days.

On completion of this, the marketing deck is created, including the sensitivity analysis, business plan, and expected returns. There is an investor conference call and the operator starts to raise equity. Investors reserve their spot, review the PPM, sign, and fund. This takes about six weeks. After funds have been received, the property closes two to three weeks later. The distributions start about sixty days later.

21. How will the operator communicate with me?

You will receive monthly updates via email on progress of the investments. The operator will identify how many units were renovated, the rents collected, and other details. Quarterly property management financials will be available as well. You can also track your investment on an investor portal, which many operators offer. In March you will receive a schedule K-1 statement for your taxes.

22. What is a sensitivity analysis?

This shows different scenarios for occupancy and where the breakeven point will be if there is a decline in occupancy or if rents are not as high as projected. Fortunately, most of our scenarios allow occupancy to go down to 75% and still break even. In the 2009 financial crisis, third party data showed that in one of the submarkets in Dallas, the lowest occupancy level was 85%.

23. Are the forecasts conservative?

Absolutely. A good sponsor will be focused on preserving investor's capital and make sure they under-promise and over-deliver. Key metrics include rent projections. They should be under the top of the market after renovations. The capitalization rates should be forecasted as higher than when the asset was purchased, which is more conservative as an exit strategy.

24. What are the fees paid to the syndicator?

The returns forecasted are after all fees have been paid. The sponsor is paid an acquisition fee, which is typically 2% of the purchase price, paid on closing. This covers all of the sponsor's costs to find and acquire the deal. The other common fee is the asset management fee, which is also 2%, and is based on the monthly income/revenue from the property. This fee is for execution of the business plan and overseeing the property management. Industry averages are 1–3% for both of these fees.

25. What is a split and a waterfall?

These terms relate to the division of returns to the limited and general partners. If the split is 70/30 in favor of the LP, then the limited partner receives 70% and the general partner 30% of revenue, after the preferred return is paid. This applies to all distributions or capital events. A waterfall refers to a change in the split if a certain return is achieved, typically measured by IRR. For example, a typical split would be 70/30 then change to 50/50 once the IRR hits 15%. This rewards the sponsor for achieving a higher than expected return.

26. What is a PPM?

The Private Placement Memorandum is required by the SEC and has several parts. It tends to be 100 to150 pages long. It contains a description of the offering, the risks, and includes the partnership agreement, investment summary, and subscription agreement. The entire PPM can be daunting, and the risk section can be alarming (similar to a Surgeon General's warning) by highlighting every possible risk that could happen. While it is true that there is risk with every investment, it's important to look at the track record of the sponsor and the history of multifamily investments in a severe downturn. Banks will not lend ten to thirty million dollars to a sponsor unless they are experienced, have a good business plan, and conservative underwriting. They will also need to have adequate insurance and have the property condition report completed by outside experts highlighting what fixes are to be made before taking over the property.

27. What kind of apartment buildings do you look for?

The best building is one that has good structure but is older and needs some cosmetic improvements. This is a "value-add" opportunity. This is typically a 1980 or 1990-era building, B class, in good neighborhoods, A/B class areas. (at the time of this writing). The operator then focuses on rebranding, new website, new property management team, and renovations of the property and units. Adding some technology like Nest thermostats, keyless entry and an Amazon locker pick-up site is appealing to the younger residents. We also focus on intangibles such as monthly gatherings that can foster a sense of community and improve retention of residents.

Chapter Seven

Roadblocks on the Path to Financial Freedom

Now that you know all about syndication investing in real estate and understand that this same concept applies to other types of real estate such as self-storage, mobile home communities, and even retail or industrial parks, I would like to focus next on some obstacles you may encounter.

Problem 1: Lifestyle Creep, aka Jonesitis

Since doctors are older when we get out of school, and make a good salary right away, we often fall into the trap of living a lifestyle that is technically affordable, but does not help us generate wealth. We have deprived ourselves of so much and have worked so hard that it's difficult not to buy into the notion. We are doctors and we deserve to have a nice house, a fancy car, and all of the trimmings. We end up suffering from lifestyle creep: gradually purchasing more and more stuff and spending the overhead that goes with it. When you buy a large house, not only is it expensive, but it's a hell of a lot more expense and work to keep up. There are the property taxes, home insurance, higher electricity, and gas bills to start with. But don't forget about the help you need to make the place look nice: a gardener and a housekeeper are generally needed (most of us don't want to clean a 3000-plus square-foot house with its four-plus bathrooms on our weekends). If you are in a community with amenities, there's the dreaded HOA. Oh, and if you have a pool, tack on some more for the upkeep and costs to keep it warm. Once we have kids we want the best education possible for them. This includes the best preschools and private grade schools, a minimum of $10K per year in Southern California.

Literally before you realize it, you have a monthly expense, just to keep the lights on, that is so much larger than your residency income it makes your head spin. Yes, you make a good living. Then again if you want to take some nice vacations, have a nice wardrobe, and eat out sometimes you are noticing that maybe you don't have much leftover at the end of the month. Hopefully there is enough to max out your 401(k), and you can take solace in that.

It's clear that physicians making over $250K—the starting wage for primary care physicians—need to be saving more of their money for retirement. That's easier said than done once you get on a path that leads you to a certain lifestyle with all of the accoutrements. Suddenly you realize that you need to work your ass off to maintain it and try to save with the limited runway of thirty years. It's like being on a hamster wheel, running and running, but not getting anywhere.

Problem 2: The Wild and Wooly West of Investing Outside of Wall Street

If you are fortunate enough to have some money left over after maxing out your 401(k) and profit-sharing plan, what do you do with this money?

Doctors are good at learning information. We assimilate it and store it dutifully. This serves us very well in medicine. Most of us are not out there inventing the next surgical procedure or new drug. We take what others have proven and use it.

When it comes to investing, we often take the same approach. If you ask your trusted financial advisor what you should do with your money, he will advise you of the benefits of funds and other paper assets in his arsenal. Most of these will be tied to the stock market. He or she is just telling you what they know. They have not been taught about alternative investments, so really should not advise you on them. Doctors are so busy that they are unlikely to do research on the myriad opportunities for investing that are out there. There are also the doctors who are adventurous in their investing. They are well aware that they have some serious ground to make up and want to swing for the fences with opportunities that promise big returns—maybe ten times their money—but have a significant risk of losing it all.

Most people know that, if done correctly, real estate is a solid investment. The rub is *how* to invest in real estate. We discussed earlier that there are many options for investing in real estate and most of them require a significant time commitment. There is an important question that must be asked at this juncture.

Figuring Out the Highest and Best Use of Your Time

I look at this from a macro and micro level. On the macro level, you went to school for many years of grueling training and spent a ton of money to become a doctor, a very well-paid position. It makes sense for you to spend your working time seeing patients. That is what you are paid for. On the micro level, at the office, you should be seeing patients. You should not be spending as much time on the computer as you did with the patient, not filling out endless forms for insurances. Maximizing your income means being efficient in the office, but what you do outside of the office matters too.

Burnout is a major problem in our profession. Fifty percent of physicians have at least one symptom of burnout and physician suicide is at an alarming high. One doctor commits suicide in the U.S. every day, the highest suicide rate of any profession. The number of doctor suicides—28 to 40 per 100,000—is more than twice that of the general population, new research shows. The rate in the general population is 12.3 per 100,000. These findings were presented at the American Psychiatric Association (APA) 2018 annual meeting.

Some of the most common causes of burnout are lack of autonomy and overwork. When you work long hours and feel that you don't have control over your life, you feel like crap. You lose interest in your job, you stop having empathy for your patients, and you wonder if you are really making a difference. This is a danger zone. If you are feeling any of these symptoms, please go to online to take a free Maslach burnout inventory test.

I feel very strongly that a huge reason for burnout in doctors is financial. For all of the reasons mentioned above, many of us are not financially free. We feel the burden of responsibility on our back and aren't sure what to do except keep putting one foot in front of the other, one day at a time. We aren't really living our lives to the fullest. We are not as present for our children, family, and friends as we could be.

End Goal Financial Freedom: The Holy Grail

The definition of financial freedom: basic expenses are covered even if you cannot work; the amount needed to "keep the lights on" and living in your home.

When you are financially free, you can take off the heavy anchor you've been carrying around and start enjoying life. You can work less, taking your paid, or unpaid, time off. You can take time to travel, take the adventures you desire now, instead of waiting for retirement. If possible, you can take "mini-retirements" of one to six months during this time. This has been shown to make employees happier and more productive on their return to work.

Here's another important concept to remember: the patients will always be there. They will always be there, waiting for you when you return. Just like the mail, which never stops, patients will always need doctors. I vividly remember this advice. I was in my early thirties and experienced an early miscarriage. I had been trying to get pregnant for almost a year and was distraught. I saw my OBGYN and I asked her if I should work that day. She looked me straight in the eye and said, "The patients will always be there, sweetie. You need to take care of yourself. Take today off, maybe even tomorrow. You cannot help others if you don't help yourself first." I was loath to cancel on patients but took her advice and rested for a few days.

The truth of her advice became clear to me several years later when I did get pregnant and took a three-month maternity leave. The world did not end. My patients received great care from my colleagues. My colleagues managed my workload. Everything was fine. Fine! Me not being there for three months was a drop in the bucket of time. I don't think most people in the company even realized I was gone!

I see this now. When another doctor takes a leave for a few months, there is a time of increased work at first, but this slows down to a trickle after a few weeks. Then it's not a big deal, and the time they are absent goes quickly; we have business as usual.

When you are financially free, you can make decisions about where and how much you want to work that come from your heart not from a need to make a certain salary. This gives you the freedom to enjoy practicing in your field at the level that gives you joy. The pressure is gone, and you can design your medical practice around your life.

In short, you can get off that damn noisy plastic hamster wheel and start driving the luxury bus that represents your life.

Okay, you might say, I get it. I can take time off of work and the world will not end. But how the hell can I do this? I've got a lot of bills to pay! I get it. I get small-minded when I am worried about money, when I stare at the Netflix bill and want to cancel it. Because cutting $11.99 from my monthly budget is definitely going to help? No, we need to switch from a mindset of scarcity, of lack, of not enough (time or money) to the opposite. We need to have an abundance mindset. Think of ways to grow the proverbial pie. Increasing your net worth in a linear, incremental line is a recipe for years of nose-to-the-grindstone work. We want to increase our net worth exponentially, which will create a life of freedom and time, leaving a legacy for the next generation.

It's so important for us to live our lives now, while we are young(ish) and (mostly) healthy. Remember that the goal is not necessarily retirement. If you have a sweet balance between work, time off, mini retirements, and vacation, then what is retirement anyway? If you love doing the work of medicine on your own terms, then retirement may not be a word in your vocabulary. Or if you really want to hang up the stethoscope after you reach financial freedom, go for it. If you want to retire from paid medicine and work on missions around the world using your valuable skills, more power to you. The point is that you should be the one to design your life, and you have the knowledge and the skills to do it.

What is your journey? If you want to be financially free, put your hard-earned money to work for you. It will create passive income while you are sleeping, travelling, relaxing, or spending time with your loved ones. Then you have the ability to decide what matters most to you. What kind of impact can you make in the world when you can look beyond the myopic view most of us have? When we are worried about our bills, our stuff, and our income we are self-centered. We have to be.

When this tremendous pressure is gone, what might you be inspired to do in the community, or the world?

Chapter Eight

RBA: Risks, Benefits, and Alternatives

I hope that you get a feel for my passion to have you live a life that you've designed, not just one that you were handed when you decided to start medical school. I fervently wish that I knew more of this when I first started out. Actually, I did read *Rich Dad, Poor Dad* and the *Cashflow Quadrant* by Robert Kiyosaki when I was about five years into my career. If you haven't read them, I highly recommend them both (after you finish this book). Disclaimer: I was a big fan and paid a few hundred dollars to attend a daylong seminar by Rich Dad and was sorely disappointed when it was clear from the beginning that they were there to upsell very expensive programs, in the $30–$50K range.

If you're a doctor, you're undoubtedly familiar with the Risks Benefits and Alternatives approach to discussing treatment options with patients. Let's apply this to investing as well.

Assessing the Risks

The biggest question on investors' minds: How risky is this and will I lose my money?

Humans hate to lose. We hate losing more than we love winning. We are wired to protect ourselves from losses more than to seek gains. This has been coined "loss aversion." In cognitive psychology and decision theory, loss aversion refers to people's tendency to prefer avoiding losses to acquiring equivalent gains: it is better to not lose $100 than to find $100. The principle is very prominent in the domain of economics.

To this end, we need to respect that part of us that is unwilling to take chances and lose money. I am a champion at loss aversion. I am so cheap that I hate to gamble; the idea of putting my hard-earned money into a machine or on a game table to have it just disappear, for nothing more than a brief moment of entertainment, disgusts me. I hate bingo, lottery tickets, even raffles (unless it's for a good cause, of course).

So back to real estate. There was a big problem in the real estate market around 2007. Many of you will remember this. Our homes were commonly being treated as both our ATMs and our retirement savings, but absolutely plummeted in value almost overnight. The Dow Jones Industrial Average, a stock market index that indicates the value of thirty large, publicly owned companies based in the United States, hit a market low of 6,469.95 on March 6, 2009, having lost over 54% of its value since the October 9, 2007 high. Ripples were felt through our economy, and the world.

Conversely, the data from NAREIT (National Association of REIT) on returns in REIT sectors over 2007-2009, a reflection of the real estate market, showed that returns of Mobile Homes were 0.47%, self-storage -3.8% and apartments were -6.72%. Retail and industrial REIT sectors dropped -8.16 and -12.32% respectively.

While there are no guarantees and past performance is not necessarily indicative of future performance, certain sectors of real estate have been shown to be more resistant to recessions than others.

Tenants, Termites, and Toilets. As outlined earlier in the book, taking care of a single-family home is not passive at all. Managing all of the aspects of an investment home is work, and if the responsibility is handed over to a property manager, you still have to watch over them. On top of that, of course, you are financially responsible for the maintenance of the home. The bane of landlords everywhere are "The Three Ts"—Tenants, Termites and Toilets.

Trust, Team, and Track Record: The New Three T's

So how do you select a solid operator? Before I investigate a new potential deal's worthiness by checking out the location, the underwriting, returns, hold time, business plan, and all of the other juicy details, I look into the one factor that is of utmost importance: the operator.

The biggest risk by far with investing in syndication real estate is *implementation of the business plan*. It doesn't matter if the glossy investment summary looks beautiful and the numbers pencil perfectly if none of that occurs due to poor implementation.

Trust. How do you trust someone that you don't know? A quick Google search goes a long way. Check LinkedIn and Facebook and read any articles the key sponsors have written. I investigated my first deal by digging around on the internet, even doing a criminal background check. This is a well-regulated industry and things like bankruptcies, felonies, litigation, or SEC violations will be red flags. I like to speak with the operator, hear them on the recorded conference call, and check out their web page. If they have been on podcasts, listen to them. Hearing someone talk can give you a great feel for their personality. I also met the operator in person for my first deal; that was a great gut check for me.

How responsive are they to investor questions? Are they available to answer questions in laymen's terms? You should be able to contact the sponsor directly, by email or phone, and get answers you are comfortable with. How often do they update investors on a deal? You can ask for previous communications and inquire about their schedule for notifying investors. Typically, there are monthly updates and quarterly financials for your review. You should be able to view the property if they have taken possession and speak with the property manager.

Ask for references of other investors who have invested in previous deals, preferably several deals and for at least a few years. You can ask how they have performed compared to projections. As well as ask how they address investor concerns.

Track Record. It is so important to review the operators' track record. It is sometimes hard to find an exit, a deal that they have completed, as we are looking at five-year turnarounds for many deals. However, if you can see how their current deals are faring, that is a good litmus test. Some operators are new and may not have more than a few deals. It is helpful if they are partnering with someone with more experience and a good track record.

Team. Being a syndication real estate operator is not a one-man (or woman) show. A team is needed to make such a massive project a success. The core General Partnership is usually comprised of several individuals, typically two to three. It is very common to bring in additional partners to help raise the needed funds for the down payment and the capital expenditures that make it a successful project. So, there are usually a few core team members, and the property management company, that are going to be involved in the day-to-day operations as the business plan unfolds. This is of critical importance and I like to review the track record of the property manager as well.

So back to risks, how likely am I to lose my money? Capital Preservation is at the very tippy-top of the list for any good operator. If an operator loses an investor's money, their career is *over*. This type of investment is very different from speculative investments. I have a friend who is raising funds for a Broadway show. They are doing a syndication, raising millions. The expectations are completely different. If the show is a hit, they can expect ten to twenty times on their funds over several years, but if it is just mediocre, or a flop, they are likely to lose all of their money.

Since a real estate investment is backed by real property, not just an idea or a product that may or may not be successful, the chances of losing your initial capital investment are extremely remote. Even if the economy hit another major recession, there is still a property backing up your funds. If values go down, the operator can just hold the asset for longer and sell at a more favorable time. If a natural disaster hits the area, this can certainly impact projected returns, but insurance will cover damage, and the asset is still there. Although common sense can come into play, I do avoid investing in mobile home parks in hurricane prone areas.

Really, the only way I see to actually lose your initial invested capital would be if the operator was a true crook, if they took your money, pocketed it and made for the Caymans. Hence the due diligence on the operator as discussed earlier. Even *if* there was a scam operator out there, they would know that this was a one-time heist. With the connectivity we all have, they would never be successful in another project again.

Adding Up the Benefits

Let's dig into the benefits of syndication-real-estate investing. Most of us know the general benefits of real estate; it's been drilled into us since we were children. Owning a home is the American Dream and considered essential for so many reasons. Land is a solid investment and provides some great tax benefits, too.

While that is easy to understand, when you are a limited partner in a syndication you own a small piece of a property and you *also* receive the benefits of being a property owner. Here is a framework based on work done by Brian Adams, where he lays out why real estate is an IDEAL investment.

> **I= Income**
> **D= Depreciation**
> **E= Equity**
> **A= Appreciation**
> **L= Leverage**
>
> **&**
>
> **T= Tax Advantaged**
> **P= Performing Asset**
> **S= Scale**

Income: This is the Holy Grail: passive income. Investing in apartments, self-storage, or mobile home parks generates income from the rents collected less expenses. These investments typically pay distributions monthly or quarterly, based on the preferred return, which ranges from 7-10%. The preferred return is paid to the limited partners before the general partners are paid.

Depreciation: As a limited partner, you benefit from depreciation of the building, which reduces taxable income. Many syndicators utilize accelerated depreciation techniques as well.

Equity: As the loan is paid down and improvements are made to the property, rents are raised which increases income. This creates more equity in the property.

Appreciation: Waiting for the market to improve is not the type of appreciation we refer to in the commercial space. That is the type of appreciation that most residential real estate, fewer than five units, relies upon. We want to *force appreciation.*

The business plan for these assets is most often to improve them (value-add) by doing renovations, creating efficient processes and providing additional services. This in turn increases the income of the property. Since these asset classes base the value of the property on the Net Operating Income (NOI), when the income goes up so does the value of the property. This is exponential because the market value = NOI/capitalization rate (%). The capitalization rate is simply what investors should expect to earn if they paid all cash for an asset. Example: if an apartment costs one million dollars and the cap rate is 6%, then the investor should expect to get 6% annually or a return of $60K, from the investment.

Please reference the example in Chapter Five, forcing appreciation, page 66.

Leverage: Sometimes we think of leverage as a bad thing, something to be avoided, especially if we were "over-leveraged" during the downturn of 2007-2009.

However, leverage is a very powerful tool in real estate that can be wielded carefully to produce phenomenal returns.

Here is an example to illustrate the power of leverage. If I bought a $5,000,000 apartment building for cash and the building generated a NOI of $300,000 a year that would be a 6% return. Alternatively, I could purchase this property with 20% down (one million). If we added value improving the NOI by 50% to both buildings to $450,000, the all cash return would be 9%, or $450K/5 million invested. Not bad, but on the leveraged property, my new NOI would be $450,000/year, less new debt payment of $225,000/year to come to a NOI of $225,000. However, $225,000 divided by $1,000,000 down payment = 22.5% return on the investment versus 9% on the all-cash deal.

This is the power of leverage.

	All Cash	Leverage 80%
Value of Apartment	$5,000,000	$5,000,000
Cash Down	$5,000,000	$1,000,000
Debt	0	$4,000,000
Payment (annual)	0	$225,000
Net Operating Income	$450,000	$450,000
Return on Investment	9%	22.5%

Tax Advantaged: High earning professionals have to be concerned with taxes. Fortunately, investing in real estate is a highly tax-efficient investment, even for a limited partner. It's not uncommon for the annual distributions to investors of 8% to be listed on the annual Schedule K-1 tax statement as a lower amount than was received, or even show a paper loss. This is because not only depreciation but also property taxes and interest on the loan can be deducted from the income.

Especially during the early years of an investment, the accelerated depreciation and expenses will reflect a significant loss on the annual Schedule K-1 tax statement. This amount is often 40-60% of the amount invested. The distributions received will be much lower than this (7 or

8% preferred return). Therefore the investor does not typically pay taxes on these distributions. For example, if $100,000 was invested, and 8% preferred return was paid out, the Schedule K-1 may have $8000 in distributions but $50,000 in losses. These losses are "passive losses" and can be used against "passive income". If there is no passive income, the losses accumulate and are "suspended". Which means that they can be used at a later date. Talk to your CPA for more information about your individual situation.

In addition, value-add syndicators frequently do a "cash-out" refinance after the renovations are complete, a few years after the property is purchased and the property's income is optimized. This refinance is considered by the IRS as a return of the investor's capital and is not a taxable event. At the time of sale—say in year five—there is some depreciation recaptured, but the expected gain at sale is considered a long-term capital gain and is treated at a lower tax rate.

Performing Asset: A performing asset is one that is already producing income. In other words, the building is in a strong market and is making money before any improvements are made. This reduces risk for the operator and the investor. Some operators like to purchase assets where there is minimal or no income, and low occupancy less than 70% as the upside can be greater if the building is turned around successfully. However, this type of investment is a lot riskier. Purchasing buildings where the occupancy is 90% or greater, and positive income already exists, allows for significant improvement to the units, building, and operations without the high risk of a non performing asset.

Scale: There are costs associated with owning buildings such as apartments that are fixed, so picking a building size that allows for economies of scale is important. The more units in a building, the lower cost-per-unit expense of maintenance would be. Once the threshold for on-site property manager and maintenance is met, the overall cost for them to manage 100 versus 200 units is about the same, but the cost per unit decreases.

Exploring the Alternatives

Yes, there are other ways to invest and get passive income other than real estate. While this book focuses on real estate, I wanted to give a quick shout out to a few of the many other types of investments:

- Paper assets: stocks/bonds/mutual funds
- Cash: your pillow/mattress, FDIC insured savings account or money market fund
- Hard money: the bank, notes, bridge loans
- Life insurance policies: infinity banking, universal life
- Private Placements: this could be other types of real estate like hotels, ground up development, or medical devices, start-ups, Broadway shows, you name it.
- Currencies: gold, silver, yen, cryptocurrencies (such as bitcoin)
- Commodities and futures
- And more

Chapter Nine

Location, Location, Location

The oldest adage of real estate still applies: location, location, location. Buying in the right market and submarket is so very important to the success of the deal. There are several factors to consider when looking at the location of a deal.

Demographics

The rate of growth of a location, the number of people moving to a city, is a good marker. In a market where the number of people moving to the city outnumbers the supply of housing, the basic laws of supply and demand will lead to higher rents. Looking at the area's household income is helpful, as well as the values of homes near the property. Seeing incomes that are higher than average indicates a good market/submarket.

Business

Looking for influx of businesses to an area is a great sign. When there are new company headquarters moving into town this bodes well for job growth, and subsequent population growth. It's also important to look for diversification of industries in the area, in case of a downturn in one industry.

Submarket

Within a good market, it's important to know the submarkets. This is difficult without intimate knowledge of the area. In our own city, we know that sometimes one block can be the difference between a great area and an unsafe area. Ideal areas are Class A areas with some older properties that need sprucing up, or Class B areas that are in emerging areas of the city. A helpful metric is rent growth, both historical and projected. It's nice to have a building near major freeways for convenience to schools, employment, shopping, and entertainment. It's always important to be near good school districts.

Comparables

While the price of commercial real estate is not dependent on comps as it is in residential transactions, it is nonetheless very important to see what the rental comps are for the area. Looking at rents in similar apartment complexes in a three-mile radius and targeting rents slightly lower than the competition is the goal to remain competitive. Likewise, the price per unit and cost per-square-foot should also be lower than similar buildings.

Chapter Ten

Self-Storage and Mobile Home Parks

W e have spent a lot of time reviewing the details of syndication real estate investing, mostly through the lens of multifamily (apartment) investing. I want to spend some time digging into the other two niches that I really like as well: Mobile home parks (MHP), also known as Mobile Home Communities, and self-storage.

Self-Storage: A Solid Investment

Self-storage is a unique asset class. It has a reputation for providing high yields and has been shown to be relatively resistant to recessions due to lower declines and default ratios versus other asset classes.

While still a relatively new industry that only got its start in the 1960s, self-storage has become a large industry and is rapidly gaining in popularity. The current number of self-storage facilities in the US is between 45,547 (Self-Storage Almanac, 2019) and 52,000 (Self Storage Association, 2018). Sources vary depending on definition and methodology.

Why is self-storage such a great investment? There are several reasons.

In the 60s and 70s the facilities were almost exclusively owned by mom-and-pop operators. While this is still the case, large branded chains have taken a spot in the market and are creating beautiful facilities with operational efficiencies and economies of scale. A few examples of these are CubeSmart, Public Storage, and Storage West. Publicly traded self-storage REITs have been one of the top performing sectors in recent years.

The storage facilities of old were on the outskirts of town, in a sketchy location, with drab concrete buildings with a squeaky roll up door. Oh, and they were hot as Hades or as cold as the North Pole, depending on the time of year. And don't forget the vermin—god help you if you left something precious in a cardboard box. I once returned to a storage facility to find some memorabilia from my grandparents, photos and letters, chewed up and turned into a rat's nest.

Not anymore. Now, you will find the facilities around the corner from your house as they move into urban and suburban areas. They're clean, some of them have climate control, and are secured by electronic gates and security systems. The really fancy ones are multilevel and fit right in with other urban buildings. As our population grows, the demand for storage increases.

Americans have a lot of stuff. Not only that, but they really like their stuff and are loath to get rid of it. Even with the decluttering craze à la Marie Kondo, most of us have more belongings than we have room for. And the clean, climate-controlled storage place that is pretty affordable and just down the street from where I live gives me a home for my things, so I can hang onto them just a little bit longer.

Millennials are delaying home purchases and renting apartments longer. While these apartments fit their lifestyle perfectly, they don't have the space a single-family home would offer them for their gear. Having an affordable nearby storage unit to store bicycles, snowboards, and camping gear is a perfect fit for these folks.

The income generated from the self-storage facility is a beautiful thing.

- Rents are relatively low compared to total expenses, which makes them affordable.

- Additional revenue streams can be created by providing ancillary services to the renters, including packing materials (boxes and tape), and the use of a company moving van.

- Once all of your stuff is in a storage unit, small rent increases are not likely to trigger you to spend all day Saturday moving your things to a different facility. For example, if it costs $100 for a small unit, and the rent increases by 6% to $106 per month, most tenants are not going to move for six dollars. Six dollars may not seem like much but increasing the operating income by 6% translates to a significant increase in the value of the property.

- Self-storage has excellent cash flow, typically in the 8-10% range. This cash flow is subject to the real estate deductions and benefits we discussed earlier.

Historical Asset Class Returns. According to the National Association of REIT (NAREIT) the self-storage sector produced an average annual return of 16.85% from 1984 to 2018. For comparison, here are the returns from some other REIT sectors during that same time:

Office: 12.15%
Retail: 12.04%
Industrial 12.73%
Residential: 13.00%
Apartments: 12.93%
Manufactured Homes: 13.20%
Mortgage: 10.64%
S&P 500: 7.06%
DQYDJ Calculator (https://dqydj.com/sp-500-return-calculator/)

I would encourage you to look at the data from NAREIT; there is a lot of interesting data on the Annual Index Values & Returns page of https://www.reit.com/data-research/reit-indexes/annual-index-values-returns.

Let's assume you had $200,000 to invest in 1994 and put your money equally into two investments. One investment for $100,000 in a self-storage REIT and reinvested all earnings while you put another $100,000 into the S&P 500 and reinvested all dividends. By 2017, the self-storage REIT would have grown to $4,026,413 while your S&P 500 stock fund would have grown to $532,243. Self-storage outperformed the large capitalization stocks index by a whopping $3,494,170. Now, astute investors recognize that past performance is not necessarily indicative of future performance, but this is clearly eye opening and worth further study.

The self-storage market has also shown itself to be relatively recession resistant. Looking at more numbers from NAREIT, self-storage outperformed other sectors during the recession period of 2007-2009. During this time self-storage produced an average loss of 3.8%. For comparison here are returns from the other REIT sectors during the same time period:

Office: -8.16%
Retail: -12.32%
Industrial: -18.31%
Residential: -6.43%
Apartments: -6.72%
Manufactured Homes: 0.47%
Healthcare: 4.92%
Mortgage: -19.54%
S&P 500: -22.03%
DQYDJ Calculator (https://dqydj.com/sp-500-return-calculator/)

Why has self-storage been shown to be recession resistant? During good times people buy and store too much stuff. But in the financial downturn, if they are moving into a smaller home or apartment because of foreclosure or downsizing, they will need somewhere to store the things that don't fit in their new place as a temporary measure until things look up.

The fact that Americans cherish their belongings in good times and bad bodes well for the self-storage investor!

There is a new type of storage solution where belongings are stored in "pods" that are packed at the residence and moved to a warehouse for safekeeping. Some wonder if this will be a disrupter for the more traditional walk or drive-up storage facilities. In my research, I have found that these pod style storage solutions have a specific niche; they are primarily for storing things during a move to a new location, or short-term storage. When people put their things in a storage facility, they often want some form of access to it that doesn't require an appointment with a forklift. This applies especially to those that are using their storage units as garages for their weekend warrior pursuits.

Another big opportunity was alluded to earlier: the move from mom-and-pop independent owners to institutional investors. The quality of this sector has caught the attention of the large REITs. But currently about 80% of properties remain in the hands of small, independent investors. The top six public companies control approximately 18% of the facilities. This fragmentation of the market provides an opportunity for a savvy operator to purchase a property at an attractive price, optimize the facility and once stabilized it becomes an attractive asset for a REIT to purchase. This can provide a quick exit for investors as well.

In summary, self-storage has shown solid performance over the past twenty-five years and even remained competitive during the Great Recession. With the upward trending occupancies and rental rates, as both millennials and retired folks move back into the city centers, self-storage presents a tremendous opportunity for investors to include in their portfolio.

Mobile Home Parks: Worth a Second Look

Mobile home parks have a bad reputation. I remember living in a mobile home, or trailer as we used to say, for a short time in the second grade. We were in transition, but even at that young age, I remember thinking that the hallways were strangely narrow and the doorknobs were all plastic and broke regularly. I also remember the dirt roads surrounding the park and the generally unkempt nature of the place.

When I moved to the United States, I carried my prejudice against "trailer parks" with me. However, I was surprised to see that the mobile home parks, as I was sharply instructed to refer to them as, were actually really nice. In my area of San Diego, the vast majority of MHPs are for senior use exclusively. They take great pride in their homes and often have a lovely clubhouse and a pool.

Mobile home parks, or MHPs, are very interesting. There are six reasons I like to invest in this asset class.

1. Affordable housing: MHPs provide an option for affordable housing as home prices and rents increase all over the county. Many baby boomers are retiring and will need more affordable places to live, especially those that have meager retirement savings and are reliant on their social security income.

2. Essentially fixed supply: When was the last time you saw a MHP being built? Yeah, me neither. Currently, there are about ten new MHPs being built in the entire US in a typical year. There are approximately 50,000 parks in existence. The stigma I had around MHPs is prevalent and therefore it is very tricky to get a new park approved by the city. As supplies decrease, demand increases.

3. Not so mobile: While called "mobile," these homes are anything but. Most parks rent the space to a homeowner. Therefore, the owner of the home doesn't own the land, just the home. So theoretically, if they wanted to change to another park they could. However, a quick look around a park confirms that these homes are very permanent, and the only move is the trip from the factory to the park. The cost of moving would start at $5000.

4. Returns: MHPs provide very attractive returns for the investors. The costs are low because the owner maintains the land and amenities, not the mobile homes. Many of the independent, mom-and-pop operators are tired, and have not optimized operations or raised rents to market level. Purchasing several parks in an area allows for efficiencies with one manager for two or three sites.

5. Institutional interest: Like self-storage, big money has shown interest in this asset class. Examples include Sam Zell, the Chicago based real estate magnate, and Warren Buffet, who owns

Clayton homes the largest manufacturer of mobile homes.

For ease of investing and diversification, I like to invest in MHPs as a fund. Individual parks don't lend themselves to syndication due to small numbers, but there is power in investing in a selection of parks that are diversified across several states and climates. Historically MHPs have provided investors with double-digit returns.

Chapter Eleven

Investing in Land Entitlement

What is Land Entitlement anyway?

A Permitted or paper lot can be defined as raw land that has been granted sub divisional approval by the local municipality with all land disturbance permits in hand. This allows it to be developed by a builder. In other words, dirt can be moved—it is "shovel ready." This has become a multibillion-dollar business which has grown out of the ashes of the 2008 housing crash and recession.

A bit of background: Single Family Homes are in massive demand and very expensive.

At the time of writing this (2022) there is a housing shortage in the US. Nationwide there is a deficit of at least 5 million single-family homes. Several factors are contributing to this shortage and can be categorized into three main areas.

Demand Factors

- The higher demand has been fueled by Millennials ready to buy their first home. There is a bulge in the demographics with 4.8 million people turning 30 between 2021 and 2024. They have led all generations in home buying in 2020.
- The COVID effect has noted a shift from urban to suburban areas as folks continue to work from home. They don't need to be close to the office so people want a bigger place with more space, more privacy, and less shared spaces.

Price Factors

- Things are more expensive right now. Supply chain issues have caused spikes in essential building supplies, like lumber. The cost of building a house is up 36K this year. Inflation is making itself at home as well, causing the cost of other supplies and labor to increase. Consistently low interest rates have made it possible for buyers to afford more expensive houses. The Federal Reserve has been purchasing large numbers of mortgage backed securities to keep rates low during COVID, nearly 700 billion. Near the end of 2021, they started to wind down this program.

Inventory Factors

- The supply of homes on the market is 53% lower in April 2021 compared to the prior year. Some of this can be attributed to uncertainty due to COVID and homeowners choosing to stay put rather than move. Since prices are high, some are waiting it out to see if they stabilize. The foreclosure moratoriums have reduced supply by 78% from 2020 to 2021. Another big factor is that the National Association of Home Builders have been building less homes for years—since the housing market crash in 2008. For example, the number of homes built from 2000-2009 was 27.05 million and from 2010 to 2019 it was 5.8 million. That's five times fewer homes built in the past decade than in any decade as far back as the 1960s.

New Housing Construction Trends

- With a shortage of 5 million homes and the perfect storm of factors outlined above, it isn't surprising that we can expect a lot of new housing starts. The Mortgage Bankers Association forecast new housing starts will be at 1.134 million in 2021, 1.165 million in 2022, and 1.21 million in 2023.

Housing Market Forecast

- While we don't have a crystal ball, the experts feel that there will be strong but decelerated growth into 2022. The Fed has advised they will start raising rates in 2022, but this may depend on the status of COVID.

Are we in a housing bubble?

- In 2006, the price gains were largely driven by speculation, an oversupply of homes, and loose lending practices which made home ownership (too) easy. Right now, demand is fueled by low rates, demographics, and lifestyle changes. Also, 70% of homeowners have greater than 20% equity. This will limit distressed sales. Nationwide we have an all-time high equity of 6.5 trillion dollars. In addition, Americans are saving more and our credit scores have gone up 6 points. And lastly, strict lending standards are still in place.

Land Entitlement is the way to profit from the high demand for single family homes.

Getting land ready for building is a very technical, detailed process. It requires specially trained Land Acquisition Managers (LAM), engineers, and a lot of paperwork. Maybe that's also why Entitled Lots are also considered "paper lots."

The 30,000-foot view of the process includes reviewing zoning ordinances, reviewing the building code, local laws, and initiatives. A Phase I Environmental Site Assessment (ESA) is needed. Use Permits and building permits must be obtained from the local government. Utility approval is needed from the local public utility company. The local Department of Transportation will approve building of roads for egress and ingress to the area. Any landscaping, such as a pond, also needs approval. If this sounds like a lot, that's because it is. The formal application process can take anywhere from three to eighteen months, about twelve months on average.

Wait —Don't the large national home builders (NHB) take care of this process?

- Yes! Historically the whole process, soup to nuts, was done by the NHB. However, the housing market crash of 2008 was very hard on the NHB because they had significant amounts of raw land on their books that was essentially worthless. Practically overnight the market was flooded with foreclosures and the demand for brand new builds was almost zero. In the years following, the NHB have put new corporate structures in place that severely limits the amount of raw land that can be purchased by the corporation. This drastically reduces their risk, decreases their timeline from purchase of land to sale of new homes, and they are more than happy to pay a premium for Entitled Land. They do still purchase some land but the rules and red tape make it hard for the land committees to purchase lots in a timely fashion.

Enter Trusted Third Party Operators

- As discussed above, the niche of Land Entitlement is highly specialized and Land Acquisition Managers (LAMs) are the specialists that are trained in finding, acquiring, and entitling land. These folks were previously employed almost exclusively by the NHB. Now independent, they can be much more efficient, moving quickly on opportunities. This benefits the NHB as they have relationships with the LAMs in their area and often direct them to acquire land in a needed market.

Importance of Land Purchase Agreements

- Return on investment is optimized and risk is lowered by *controlling* rather than owning real property. 95% of the National Home Builders and hedge fund buyers will not close on land until all land disturbance permits are in hand. A robust Land Purchase Agreement (LPA) is pivotal to success in this business.

How to Maximize ROI and Reduce Risk

- Return on investment is optimized when land is purchased and sold simultaneously and financial exposure is limited to soft costs, which works out to on average $1500/lot. It is possible to do a simultaneous close about 80% of the time. For larger projects, greater than 1000 lots, it's less likely and requires bridging capital.

6 Reasons I Love Investing in Land Entitlement

Find the "shovel" in the single-family home market.

- In the gold rush, the ones who profited consistently were supplying the gold diggers. Buying single-family homes for investment purposes is not practical in most markets. However, there is profit to be made by getting involved with the folks supplying Entitled Land to the NHB so that they can build more homes!

Cash Flow

- Cash is king, and Land Entitlement provides cash flow very quickly. No need to wait five years for the sale of a large asset to receive significant profits. Expect double-digit returns in the first year.

Short Term Deals

- These deals are short lived, just nine to eighteen months. It's unlikely that the market will shift significantly away from needing single-family homes in that timeframe. But if things start to change over time, you can pivot/exit as you're not locked into a five-year deal.

Asymmetric Risk/Reward

- This niche has a high profit margin and high demand. It is also conservative, as a good operator will only buy the land once they are sure it will be buildable and have a buyer in mind.

Diversify Your Portfolio

- This is less mainstream than many other real estate investments. Diversifying into various niches and asset classes reduces risk to your portfolio.

Extreme Niche

- This is a specialized market requiring highly trained local people. This is definitely not a DIY project. It requires a lot of local knowledge of the laws and inner workings of the city/municipality.

High Demand for Affordable Housing

- Helping get shovel ready land to the NHB, so that they can build homes, helps improve the critical housing shortage.

Chapter Twelve

Your Roadmap to Financial Freedom

A Step-by-Step Guide to Achieving a Six-Figure Passive Income in Eight Years

I have created a tool that allows you to see the power of investing as a limited partner in real estate to create passive streams of tax-advantaged income, improving your net worth light-years beyond what is possible with traditional paper investments.

Assumptions for this scenario:

- Invest $100K in a new real estate deal at the beginning of each year.
- Preferred return 8%
- Equity multiple of twos (doubling your money in five years, 20% cash on cash)
- Five year hold (sell asset at the end of five years).
- Reinvest all distributions and sale proceeds annually.

- No tax withholding, as taxes owed will vary widely among individuals.

Goals:

- $100K of passive income yearly.
- One Million dollars net worth.

Year 1:

Invest $100,000 as a limited partner in a syndication investment.

You receive an 8% preferred return, so have $8000 in distributions for the year. This results in a net worth at the end of the year of $108,000.

	Investment	Preferred Return	Cash Flow	Net worth (end of year)
Year 1 purchase	$100,000	$8000	$8000	$108,000

Year Two:

Invest $100,000 as a limited partner in a syndication investment. Add to this the $8000 distributions from the year before for a total investment of $108,000.

You receive an 8% preferred return, so have $8640 in distributions from year two, $8000 from year one, for a total cash flow of $16,640. This results in a net worth at the end of the year of $224,640.

	New Capital Investment	Reinvested Cash Flow	Total Investment	Preferred Return	Total Cash flow	Net worth (end of year)
Year 1 purchase	$100,000		$100,000	$8000	$8000	$108,000
Year 2 purchase	$100,000	$8000	$108,000	$8640	$16,640	$224,640

Year Three:

Invest $100,000 as a limited partner in a syndication investment. Add to this the $8000/year distributions from year one and $8640 from year two, for a total investment of $116,640. You receive 8% preferred return, so have $9331 in distributions for the year, plus $16,640 from years one and two, for a total cash flow of $25,971. This results in a net worth at the end of the year of $350,611.

	New Capital Investment	Reinvested Cash Flow	Total Investment	Preferred Return	Total Cash flow	Net worth (end of year)
Year 1 purchase	$100,000		$100,000	$8000	$8000	$108,000
Year 2 purchase	$100,000	$8000	$108,000	$8640	$16,640	$224,640
Year 3 purchase	$100,000	$16,640	$116,640	$9331	$25,971	$350,611

Year Four:

Invest $100,000 as a limited partner in a syndication investment. Add to this the $25,971 in cash flow from the previous year for a total investment of $125,971. You receive 8% preferred return, so have $10,078 in distributions for the year, plus $25,971 from years one, two, and three for a total cash flow of $36,049. This results in a net worth at the end of the year of $486,660.

	New Capital Investment	Reinvested Cash Flow	Total Investment	Preferred Return	Total Cash flow	Net worth (end of year)
Year 1 purchase	$100,000		$100,000	$8000	$8000	$108,000
Year 2 purchase	$100,000	$8000	$108,000	$8640	$16,640	$224,640
Year 3 purchase	$100,000	$16,640	$116,640	$9331	$25,971	$350,611
Year 4 purchase	$100,000	$25,971	$125,971	$10,078	$36, 049	$486,660

Year Five:

Invest $100,000 as a limited partner in a syndication investment. Add to this the $36,049 in cash flow from the previous year for a total investment of $136,049. You receive 8% preferred return, so have $10,884 in distributions for the year, plus $36,049 from years one, two, three and four for a total cash flow of $46,933.

At the end of year five the sale of year one assets occur, returning your original $100K investment and $60K in equity. Since the investment doubles, 2X equity multiple, over five years, the projected total is $200K with return of equity. However, since $8000 was distributed yearly for five years, $8000 x five years = $40K resulting in $60K of equity. This results in a net worth at the end of the fifth year of $693,593.

	New Capital Investment	Reinvested Cash Flow	Total Investment	Preferred Return	Return of Principal on sale	Equity sale earnings	Total Cash flow	Net worth (end of year)
Year 1 purchase	$100,000		$100,000	$8000			$8000	$108,000
Year 2 purchase	$100,000	$8000	$108,000	$8640			$16,640	$224,640
Year 3 purchase	$100,000	$16,640	$116,640	$9331			$25,971	$350,611
Year 4 purchase	$100,000	$25,971	$125,971	$10,078			$36,049	$486,660
Year 5 purchase	$100,000	$36,049	$136,049	$10,884	$100,000	$60,000	$46,933	$693,593

Year Six:

Here's where the magic starts to happen.

Invest $100,000 as a limited partner in a syndication investment. Add to this the $46,933 in cash flow from year five and the return of principal and equity from year one ($160K) for a total investment of $306,933. You receive 8% preferred return, so have $24,555 in distributions for the year, plus $38,933 from years two, three, four and five for a total cash flow of $63,487.

At the end of year six the sale of year two asset occurs, returning your $108K investment and $64,800 in equity. This results in a net worth at the end of the year of $921,880.

	New Capital Investment	Reinvested Cash Flow	Reinvested principal and equity	Total Investment	Preferred Return	Return of Principal on sale	Equity sale earnings	Total Cash flow	Net worth (end of year)
Year 1 purchase	$100,000			$100,000	$8000			$8000	$108,000
Year 2 purchase	$100,000	$8000		$108,000	$8640			$16,640	$224,640
Year 3 purchase	$100,000	$16,640		$116,640	$9331			$25,971	$350,611
Year 4 purchase	$100,000	$25,971		$125,971	$10,078			$36,049	$486,660
Year 5 purchase	$100,000	$36,049		$136,049	$10,884	$100,000	$60,000	$46,933	$693,593
Year 6 purchase	$100,000	$46,933	$160,000	$306,933	$24,555	$108,000	$64,800	$63,487	$921,880

Year Seven:

Invest $100,000 as a limited partner in a syndication investment. Add to this the $63,487 in cash flow from year six and the return of principal and equity from year one ($172,800) for a total investment of $336,287. You receive 8% preferred return, so have $26,903 in distributions for the year, plus $58,489 from years three through six for a total cash flow of $81,750.

At the end of year seven the sale of year three asset occurs, returning your $116,640 investment and $69,984 in equity. This results in a net worth at the end of the year of $1,173,615.

	New Capital Investment	Reinvested Cash Flow	Reinvested principal and equity	Total Investment	Preferred Return	Return of Principal on sale	Equity sale earnings	Total Cash flow	Net worth (end of year)
Year 1 purchase	$100,000			$100,000	$8000			$8000	$108,000
Year 2 purchase	$100,000	$8000		$108,000	$8640			$16,640	$224,640
Year 3 purchase	$100,000	$16,640		$116,640	$9331			$25,971	$350,611
Year 4 purchase	$100,000	$25,971		$125,971	$10,078			$36,049	$486,660
Year 5 purchase	$100,000	$36,049		$136,049	$10,884	$100,000	$60,000	$46,933	$693,593
Year 6 purchase	$100,000	$46,933	$160,000	$306,933	$24,555	$108,000	$64,800	$63,487	$921,880
Year 7 purchase	$100,000	$63,487	$172,800	$336,287	$26,903	$116,640	$69,984	$81,750	$1,173,615

Year Eight:

Invest $100,000 as a limited partner in a syndication investment. Add to this the $81,750 in cash flow from year seven and the return of principal and equity from year two ($186,624) for a total investment of $368,374. You receive 8% preferred return, so have $29,470 in distributions for the year, plus $72,419 from years four through seven for a total cash flow of $101,889.

At the end of year eight the sale of year four asset occurs, returning your $125,971 investment and $75,583 in equity. This results in a net worth at the end of the year of $1,451,087.

	New Capital Investment	Reinvested Cash Flow	Reinvested principal and equity	Total Investment	Preferred Return	Return of Principal on sale	Equity sale earnings	Total Cash flow	Net worth (end of year)
Year 1 purchase	$100,000			$100,000	~~$8000~~			$8000	$108,000
Year 2 purchase	$100,000	$8000		$108,000	~~$8640~~			$16,640	$224,640
Year 3 purchase	$100,000	$16,640		$116,640	~~$9331~~			$25,971	$350,611
Year 4 purchase	$100,000	$25,971		$125,971	$10,078			$36,049	$486,660
Year 5 purchase	$100,000	$36,049		$136,049	$10,884	$100,000	$60,000	$46,933	$693,593
Year 6 purchase	$100,000	$46,933	$160,000	$306,933	$24,555	$108,000	$64,800	$63,487	$921,880
Year 7 purchase	$100,000	$63,487	$172,8001	$336,287	$26,903	$116,640	$69,984	$81,750	$1,173,615
Year 8 purchase	$100,000	$81,750	$186,624	$368,674	$29,470	$125,971	$75,583	$101,889	$1,451,087

Initial Goals:

- $100K of passive income yearly.
- One million dollars net worth..
- By the end of year eight you have $101,889 in passive income and a net worth of 1.45 million dollars.

Years Nine–Twelve (and Beyond)

Now things start to get crazy. As you continue to sell assets and reinvest, your net worth and cash flow increase by leaps and bounds, reaching a net worth of $3,217,420 and cash flow of $221,955 by the end of year twelve.

	New Capital Investment	Reinvested Cash Flow	Reinvested principal and equity	Total Investment	Preferred Return	Return of Principal on sale	Equity sale earnings	Total Cash flow	Net worth (end of year)
Year 8 purchase	$100,000	$81,750	$186,624	$368,674	$29,470	$125,971	$75,583	$101,889	$1,451,087
Year 9 purchase	$100,000	$101,889	$201,554	$403,443	$32,275	$136,049	$81,629	$124,087	$1,756,803
Year 10 purchase	$100,000	$124,087	$217,678	$441,765	$35,341	$306,933	$184,160	$148,544	$2,189,507
Year 11 purchase	$100,000	$148,544	$491,092	$739,637	$59,171	$336,287	$201,772	$183,161	$2,674,440
Year 12 purchase	$100,000	$183,161	$538,060	$821,220	$65,698	$368,374	$221,025	$221,955	$3,217,420

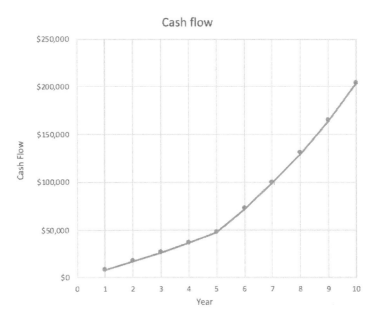

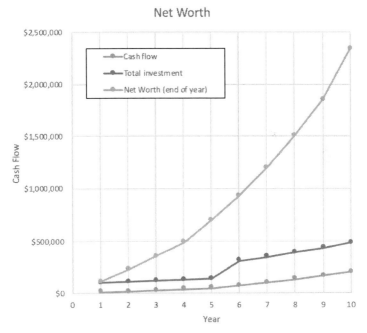

At this point you can also stop adding new capital. If you invest for eight years, ($800,000) and then stop investing new capital, you can see your net worth continue to escalate.

	New Capital Investment	Reinvested Cash Flow	Reinvested principal and equity	Total Investment	Preferred Return	Return of Principal on sale	Equity sale earnings	Total Cash flow	Net worth (end of year)
Year 8 purchase	$100,000	$81,750	$186,624	$368,674	$29,470	$125,971	$75,583	$101,889	$1,451,087
Year 9 purchase	$0	$101,889	$201,554	$303,443	$24,275	$136,049	$81,629	$116,087	$1,648,803
Year 10 purchase	$0	$116,087	$217,678	$333,765	$26,701	$306,933	$184,160	$131,904	$1,964,867
Year 11 purchase	$0	$131,904	$491,092	$622,997	$49,840	$336,287	$201,772	$157,189	$2,323,829
Year 12 purchase	$0	$157,189	$538,060	$695,249	$55,620	$368,374	$221,025	$185,906	$2,730,760

For Extra Credit

Go to my website vmdinvesting.com/roadmap to download the Roadmap to Financial Freedom Blueprint, utilized in the scenario above. You can adjust the amount invested annually, the returns, and project your cash flow and net worth up to twenty years. See where you reach your crossover point into financial freedom!

Chapter Thirteen

When Should I Invest?

This is one of the biggest questions I hear people ask. The answer really depends on which "when" you are referring to.

"When" Question #1: Where are we in the real estate cycle and should I invest now, or wait until prices go down? Up until 2007, it was unthinkable that prices would go down, but then it happened and the market tanked, taking our retirement plans with it. However, since then prices have steadily increased and while the year over year increases have slowed, and even flattened in some areas, without a crystal ball it is impossible to know when or if prices will actually go down.

We do appear to be late in a cycle, and predictably prices correct in this phase. However, sitting on the sidelines and waiting for an event that may not ever occur will not help you become financially free. Investing smartly in solid deals with conservative underwriting in recession resistant niches is still a good bet, even late in the market cycle.

"When" Question #2: When should I invest in relation to the milestones in my life? This one is a biggie.

Anne graduated from her cardiology residency at age 34 with $150K in debt. She is married, has two children in preschool, ages two and four. She and her husband have been living in a two-bedroom apartment during her schooling. He works as an IT administrator and makes a good living, $75K per year. She is now working full time at a practice with several other cardiologists and has a salary guarantee for $450K for her first year in practice.

She is so dang tired of pinching pennies and living in their cramped apartment. They move into a nice home and pay more than they had budgeted, because as they looked around the realtor kept inching them toward more expensive properties, and before they knew it their "ceiling" of $350K had gone up to $500K because they "qualified." As they have minimal savings, they get into the home with only 5% down. The home is beautiful, and the neighbors are so nice! But gosh they drive nice cars. Turns out the schools locally are just okay, and Anne learns quickly from her well-meaning neighbors that the private school is really the only thing to do. Of course, her kids are in a very nice preschool that is $1500 for both kids with the aftercare. And her lovely new home needs furnishings for more rooms than she can fathom. Her 15-year-old Nissan still runs well but feels out of place in her manicured driveway and interest rates are so low! She purchases a new BMW SUV, the nicest car she has ever had by far.

She loves her new job and is thriving, but the work is very demanding, and she finds herself at the hospital or the office into the evenings. She keeps meaning to sign up for the 401(k) plan to automatically deduct from her checks and she thinks that she is eligible for profit sharing, whatever that is. There is also something about a health savings account, (I), that she needs to look into.

She throws herself into her practice, learning the ropes of a new system and building up her patient base. When she comes up for air six months later, she is distressed to see that the money left over after expenses are paid is much smaller than she expected. After paying taxes, student loan debt, mortgage, preschool, car payments, and credit cards that were used for furnishing the house, she cannot believe how little remains. She is embarrassed to note that she doesn't even have an emergency fund and is not sure that she can fund her 401(k) this year, let alone her HSA or profit sharing.

While this story about Anne may seem a little extreme, I am surprised by how many physicians with incomes in the robust six figures are just not saving.

My advice to the young physicians out there, advice I wish I had known when I was a new grad:

Resist the siren song of the automatic lifestyle adjustment you feel you deserve upon graduation and being hired to earn the big bucks. You've lived on a low income for years, so you know you can do it. Now that you earn good money, you can certainly treat yourself, but don't make yourself a slave to your debt and expenses. This makes your new job a pair of golden handcuffs, which feels terrible.

As physicians, we are in the unique position of being accredited investors, by and large, directly out of school. The population of the US that is accredited investors is about 6% at the time of this writing. That means that you earn more than 94% of the population.

Being an accredited investor allows you to invest in private placements, like syndications, that 94% of the population *does not have access to!*

This is the secret sauce of wealth: those that have access to these investments have an unfair advantage over the average American. They can invest their money and receive double-digit returns on their money. While those who are limited to Wall Street have had an average of 8% returns over the past twenty-four years.

Many people understand intuitively that real estate is a great investment, backed by a physical property. This gives it security compared to Wall Street. Investing in real estate as an individual is generally imagined to be purchasing single-family homes and renting them out, or buying and flipping homes. As discussed earlier in the book, this plan is anything but passive from start to finish. But if you have limited capital, this may be the only way to make your fortune in real estate.

Here is the thing, listen carefully. As accredited investors, you can *skip* ahead in line about ten to fifteen years and start investing in large multifamily properties of 100, 200, 300 units right out of the gate. Are you buying the 60-million-dollar property yourself? Of course not, you're a full-time doctor working hard! But when you are young and early in your career, if you can start investing in real estate in this way and commit to investing over the first five years of your career, you have just paved your own road to financial freedom.

Imagine you have a student loan payment of $1500 per month. You assume that you cannot start investing until you have paid off your debt. If you have a loan term of ten years, then that is a very long time to start investing, especially if you're in your 30s already.

Daniel completes his residency in internal medicine and plans to work as a hospitalist, earning $450K per year. He is married, with two young children. He has $150K in student debt. They live in a small two-bedroom apartment and his wife works as a teacher and earns $75K per year.

Upon graduation they relocate to be near his hospital. He has a ten-minute commute and they are renting a small house until they get to know the area. Daniel and his wife have decided that they want to start investing before accumulating any more debt and have been busy learning about opportunities in real estate. His 15-year-old Toyota 4Runner is working just fine and he opts to keep it for a while. Fortunately, the public schools in the neighborhood are excellent and his wife works at one of them, so they don't need aftercare.

Keeping expenses low, they soon have $25K they can invest in a real estate syndication. The 8% preferred return pays a meager $133/month, and his buddies from the hospital think he is a little crazy. But he is able to save $150K per year and invest in various properties, in different states and markets. After a year he has $1000 per month in passive cash flow, and after two years he has $2000 per month. At this point, the passive income will pay the student loan payments. Depending on the interest rate for his loan, he may opt to pay off the student loan quicker with the passive cash flow or reinvest the leftover cash.

Purchasing a home can be looked at in a similar way. Your own home does not produce income like investment real estate. While it is considered an asset by the banks, it really takes money out of your pocket, not only to pay the mortgage but also the taxes, insurance, and maintenance. It is easy to become cash poor when you have a large home to maintain. If you can develop a robust stream of passive income early in your career, you could have enough to pay for your mortgage as well, ditto for car payments.

My advice is to not take on any additional debt until you have passive cash flow to help you make the payments. This approach will create a wealth snowball over eight to ten years. As the properties refinance or sell, you will receive large checks with the earned equity and return of your principal, which can be utilized to invest in another deal, wipe out the car debt or make a big dent in the student loans.

Chapter Fourteen

Invest with Money
You've Already Saved for Retirement

O kay, you may be thinking, this all sounds fabulous, you have completely sold me on investing as a limited partner in real estate.

Wait, that means I need to have at least $25,000 just lying around!

Using Retirement Money That's Hopefully Not in Your Mattress

Even if you're just getting started and are planning on taking some of the advice given so far in this book, it may take some time to save up to fifty grand. Interestingly you may already have money to invest in real estate and not even know it! Money that is languishing in an old IRA, or another retirement account could be reallocated to a new investment. Many of you have access to retirement funds to invest in real estate. Money that is currently fluctuating with the whims of the stock market can be transferred to a self-directed retirement plan, allowing you to take control of your savings and create wealth through real estate.

If you have an IRA or any money in your 401(k) that was rolled over from a previous employer, you can transfer these funds to either a self-directed

IRA or 401(k). This allows you to invest this money in any variety of investments, including but not limited to the stock market. Here are a few options for investing in a self-directed plan:

- Syndications
- Real estate (worldwide): apartments, single family homes, commercial property, land
- US Gold and Silver Bullion coins or bars
- Business startups
- Tax lien certificates
- Notes
- Securities
- CDs
- Stocks, bonds, mutual funds
- Commodities and futures
- And more!

The ideal retirement plan is a self-directed (sometimes called solo) 401(k) because you have true checkbook control of your money and invest as you see fit. With a self-directed IRA you are able to invest in real estate and other transactions as listed above, but you have a third-party custodian that needs to approve your investments. That can cause significant delays. Also, self-directed IRAs are subject to UBIT, Unrelated Business Tax Income, a sneaky tax that gets triggered by investments that have debt involved (as most real estate does). There are several companies that provide services to help get you set up with a self-directed plan. These plans were traditionally for the small business owner. However, you can still qualify for one of these plans even if you do not have a small business. If you have a side gig, some part-time income, or even your real estate investment business, then you can have a self-directed plan.

The best part of being in control of your money is that you can take it out of Wall Street. Take it away from the fund managers that have been making decisions about your money, decisions that may be profitable for them but not necessarily in your best interests.

When distributions occur for investments that are in the retirement plan, all go back into the retirement bank account, including the proceeds from a sale. Imagine a large brick wall between you, the individual, and the LLC or retirement plan. And as with all retirement plans, the money grows tax free, allowing you to reinvest the full amount of the dividends from your investments.

Other benefits of a self-directed 401(k) are the maximum contributions of $56,000 per year and the ability to borrow up to $50,000 from your account. They also provide protection from creditors in lawsuits or bankruptcy and some have the ability to purchase life insurance inside the plan.

There is also an option to convert some or all of your plan to a Roth IRA, which allows you to pay taxes up front on the contribution, but the money grows tax free and is not taxed on withdrawals.

Why haven't you heard of these plans?

Well, the retirement plan industry is a monster with over twenty trillion dollars in assets as of 2019. The vast majority of this money is held in paper assets on Wall Street and the fees charged by these institutions are very profitable for them. They would rather you keep your money with one of them than take control and become your own trustee. This also means that you can take your money out of stocks, bond and mutual funds and invest in other assets as listed earlier.

This is just a brief overview to introduce the topic of qualified retirement plans. To find out if your specific situation would benefit from one of these plans and to learn more please contact one of the companies that specialize in this area and can assist you through the process.

In Conclusion

Unlock the Golden Handcuffs of
Your High Paying Job

I will share a short parable that has made the rounds over the years on esteemed websites. Every time I read it, it makes me pause and look inward. The story is often referred to as *"The Banker and the Fisherman"* or *"The Mexican Fisherman"* – and it brings a lesson in the beauty of simplicity and gratitude over blind ambition.

For those curious, the story has been adopted and modified with a decided (and appropriate) American flavor over the years, but it appears that the origin of *"The Mexican Fisherman"* story was through a short story *"Anekdote zur Senkung der Arbeitsmoral" ("Anecdote concerning the Lowering of Productivity")*, published by a German writer, Heinrich Böll, in 1963.

> A successful businessman was vacationing near a beach in Mexico. He went for a walk on the beach and came across a local man fishing by the shore. The businessman stopped to watch him fish for a time, and they talked. While they chatted, he caught four or five fish in rapid succession. Then the man started packing up to head home.

The businessman said, "Why are you quitting now? You're on a roll! The fish are really biting right now!"

The man replied, "I have caught enough to feed my family, and give some away to my friends. I don't need any more fish today."

"What are you going to do the rest of the day then?" the businessman asked.

"Well, I will take the fish home and clean them. I will spend some time playing with my children this morning, then have the fresh fish for lunch. I will take a siesta this afternoon with my wife, then go to the village square this evening to be with my friends and play my guitar."

"But," the businessman explained, "If you caught more fish then you could sell them. In fact, in short order you would need to hire some employees to help you. You would probably also need a few boats to catch more fish."

"Señor," the man replied, "where would I sell all those fish? This is a small village that would not need so many fish."

The businessman chuckled. "Well of course you would have to move. The fish would be shipped elsewhere to be sold to people all over the country. You would probably want to base your business in a large port city, like San Diego or Los Angeles. You could easily build a multimillion-dollar business!"

"But señor," the man asked wonderingly, "how long will this take?"

"Oh, twenty, twenty-five years, max," the businessman said airily.

"Why would I do that?" the man asked.

"So that you can sell the business for millions of dollars, of course!"

"But what would I do next, señor?"

"Well, with the millions from the sale you will be able to retire in comfort in a beachside town in Mexico and spend your days fishing, spending time with your children, take siestas with your wife, and go to the village to play music with your buddies in the evening," the businessman said slowly, blanching at his own words.

"Ah," replied the man. "I see. Thanks for your advice, señor. Enjoy your vacation. Maybe I will see you here in twenty years when you've retired after selling your business."

The story of the fisherman and the businessman—which has been around for many years—resonated with me because I realized that it is so important to take the time to reflect on what we are really after in life. What do you actually want? This may take some reflection. Once we get on the fast-moving train of life and career it is difficult to take a 30,000-foot view as we spend our days focusing on the minutiae. We put one foot in front of the other, moving forward, but if we don't really know where we are going we may end up somewhere we didn't intend.

Above all, we need to be intentional with our lives. The days of previous generations, where you work until you retire at 65 with a gold watch and a pension are long gone. The company doesn't take care of you anymore, with few exceptions. Since the Employee Retirement Income Security Act of 1974 (ERISA) and implementation of the 401(k), putting the responsibility of funding retirement into the hands of the workers, Americans are woefully unprepared for retirement.

As high-income professionals, you are in the small minority of folks that have the ability to fund a comfortable retirement. But what qualifies as "enough?" After I was told that I needed four million dollars to retire I researched all the many ways you can calculate what is needed for retirement. And I learned that people differ greatly in what they expect retirement to look like. This is probably one of the most intensely personal questions you can answer.

It all comes down to what do you really want, and how much do you really need?

Maybe for your retirement you plan on visiting the wonders of the world on your lengthy bucket list, but realize shortly after you begin your travels that you hate flying and sleeping in hotels. You had never traveled for more than two weeks, and after eight weeks of your year-long trip you're ready to call it quits.

Or perhaps you envision retiring on a quiet beach with a good book and a fruity drink. So you move to a sunny locale with spotty internet and the isolation you craved. Then after a month you're so bored and lonely that you're afraid your brain is turning to mush.

The lifestyle you want in retirement may take less money than you think. When your financial advisor, or the internet calculator, gives you a retirement amount that you need so that you can do the 4% safe withdrawal rate and maintain your income for thirty years, it can be daunting. But keep in mind, this is only if you are thinking, "work, work, work."

Save in paper assets. Retire. Start taking withdrawals. If you take a nonlinear approach and start creating passive income in real estate that will snowball. This investment can support you in retirement instead of having to literally save millions of dollars and hand them over to fickle Wall Street and cross your fingers. While historically stocks do give a return of 8%, there is a very important concept called "sequence of returns." If you are unlucky enough to retire when the market has losses for several years, and you start taking money out of your account, you risk spending your nest egg down to zero before you die.

Sequences of Returns Risk in the Income Phase: Losing Earlier vs. Losing Later

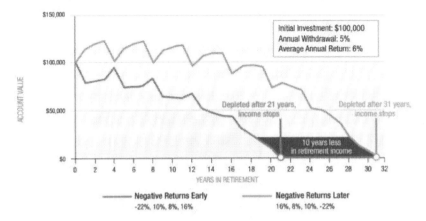

This chart is for illustrative purposes only, from the website www.selling.protective.com. It assumes an initial account value of $100,000 for a hypothetical portfolio with a sequence of returns of 16%, 8%, 10%, and -22% that repeats indefinitely and compared to the same returns in the reverse order. Both scenarios assume an annual withdrawal rate of 5% and an average annual return of 6%.

We tend to think of our lives as a linear progression. We are born, go to grade school, then college, then medical school, residency, get a job, and work until it's time to retire at the government-chosen age of sixty-five. We delay the things we want to pursue until retirement because there is no time to pursue them in the working years. We stuff our once-a-year vacations in one to two week increments, which is barely enough time to start relaxing. Oftentimes we need to cram so much into a vacation that we are more tired when we return and jump back on the treadmill. Unfortunately for many, the work that piled up when we were gone makes it doubly painful to return to our jobs.

I was able to visit Italy for two weeks this past summer and stayed with friends. While I enjoy planning vacations, this one was different. I was very busy at work and didn't have much time to review guidebooks and look at maps, so essentially, we just showed up in Italy without an itinerary. Of course, having hosts that can show you the sights was amazing, and my laissez-faire attitude wouldn't have worked without them! But I got a feel for what it would be like to have a more relaxed approach to travel. Such an approach really can only happen when you have the luxury of more time. If you haven't scheduled every day and booked hotels in different cities, you are able to go with the flow. You meet someone at a coffee shop that invites you to their home for a get together? Awesome, we will be there! Learn of a concert playing in a few days? We can make that happen!

The concept of mini-retirements, taking a sabbatical from work for up to six months is, in my opinion, the best way to experience your bucket list without waiting for retirement. You can take your family with you while they're young, enriching their lives as well as strengthening your relationship. As we know, when you've retired and your kids are in their thirties with careers and kids of their own, they aren't going to be traveling the world with you.

Travel isn't the only option, of course. I would look at each mini-retirement as a sampling of a possible lifestyle you may want to pursue when you stop working. You may want to learn a new skill, start a side business, work on a passion project, write a book, or do a mission trip with Doctors without Borders. The possibilities are endless. Central to all of this is that you are intentionally designing your life to do what is most important to you. You may not actually know what that is until you do it.

This is why passive income is so important; it allows you the freedom to explore, take some time off, get out of the office to have experiences, learn, grow and have fun! The best part is that the person you become will be a better physician because of the time spent away from the hospital or clinic. It's been shown that sabbaticals improve morale, decrease burnout, and make employees more productive.

The ability to not work and have enough passive income to cover your basic expenses is the key that unlocks the golden handcuffs of a high paying job. If you can choose how much you want to work, you may surprise yourself by working longer than you thought, because you enjoy it so much! If you have passive income and still enjoy your work on a limited scale, there may not be any reason for an official hard stop to your career.

"Choose a job you love,
and you will never have to work a day in your life."

~ Confucius

To download the free "Roadmap to Financial Freedom Blueprint," go to www.vmdinvesting.com/roadmap. This custom spreadsheet will enable you to customize how much to invest year over year and learn the power of real estate investing to reach financial freedom.

Keep in touch! Visit us on

Facebook—https://www.facebook.com/vmdinvesting

And

LinkedIn—www.linkedin.com/company/vmd-investing

If you like this book, please leave a review on Amazon!

To be notified of any updates or new editions to this book, please go to vmdinvesting.com and subscribe to our newsletter.

Introduction to VMD Investing

B uild Wealth. Experience Freedom. Leave a Legacy.

VMD Investing helps busy professionals build wealth with passive, income-producing real estate that provides double-digit returns and a proven roadmap to financial freedom.

VMD Investing is here to fast-track you towards your ideal investment opportunities. We understand how it feels to watch helplessly as the balance of your portfolio swings wildly with the whims of the market.

We focus on education and investment opportunities in real estate syndication to create strong passive income with wealth accumulation, hassle-free ownership in some of the strongest real estate niches such as **multifamily apartments, self-storage and manufactured home parks**. Our operator partners are some of the most respected and experienced in their respective niches.

We are passionate about teaching fellow professionals how they can take control of their investments and transcend the time equals money equation.

Step 1

- Sign up for the Legacy Club
- It's free and easy.

Step 2

- Connect with us
- We will contact you to learn about your goals, frustrations and current situation. We will look for resources and investments that match your goals.

Step 3

- Invest
- We will keep you informed with our investment offerings and when you see one that fits with your needs, we will guide you through the process.

Step 4

- Experience Freedom
- Congratulations, you've taken control of your investments and your money is working hard for you while you are relaxing, spending time with your family or on vacation.

If you would like to have a quick introduction so we can learn more about you, discuss our model, and share ideas, please contact me at vanessa@vmdinvesting.com to find a time to connect.

About the Author

Vanessa Peters, MD, is the founder of VMD Investing and has been investing in real estate for eleven years in single family homes, commercial retail, apartment communities, self-storage, land, and manufactured home parks. She has invested in over 3,000 units across fifteen properties and five funds.

She is passionate about helping busy professionals build wealth through passive, income-producing real estate that provides attractive returns and a proven roadmap to financial freedom.

Vanessa Peters earned her medical degree at the University of Calgary, Alberta, Canada, and moved to the US from Canada in 2002. Dr. Peters is a Family Physician and Chief Physician Officer for Graybill Medical Group, a primary-care-owned medical group in North San Diego County with twelve locations and 80-plus providers.

She is involved in her community and is on the Board of Directors for Interfaith Community Services, a nonprofit that focuses on reducing homelessness in San Diego County. She lives in Escondido with her husband and son and enjoys cooking, hiking, aviation, traveling, and yoga.

Made in the USA
Las Vegas, NV
18 November 2023

81083046R10066